ANCHORED IN HIM

ANCHORED IN HIM

Rock of our Salvation

Ulysses Tuff

WESTBOW PRESS®
A DIVISION OF THOMAS NELSON
& ZONDERVAN

Copyright © 2016 Ulysses Tuff.

All rights reserved. No part of this book may be used or reproduced by any means, graphic, electronic, or mechanical, including photocopying, recording, taping or by any information storage retrieval system without the written permission of the author except in the case of brief quotations embodied in critical articles and reviews.

All Scripture quotations are taken from the *King James Version* unless otherwise indicated.

Scripture quotations marked (NKJV) are taken from the *New King James Version®*. Copyright © 1982 by Thomas Nelson. Used by permission. All rights reserved.

Scripture quotations marked (NIV) are taken from the *Holy Bible, New International Version®*. NIV®. Copyright © 1973, 1978, 1984 by International Bible Society. Used by permission of Zondervan. All rights reserved worldwide.

Scripture quotations marked (TLB) are taken from *The Living Bible*, copyright © 1971 by Tyndale House Foundation. Used by permission of Tyndale House Publishers Inc., Carol Stream, IL 60188. All rights reserved.

Scripture quotations marked (AMP) are taken from the *Amplified*® **Bible**, Copyright © 1954, 1958, 1962, 1964, 1965, 1987 by The Lockman Foundation. Used by permission.

Scripture quotations marked (NLT) are taken from the *Holy Bible, New Living Translation*, copyright © 1996, 2004, 2007 by Tyndale House Foundation. Used by permission of Tyndale House Publishers, Inc., Carol Stream, IL 60188. All rights reserved.

WestBow Press books may be ordered through booksellers or by contacting:

WestBow Press
A Division of Thomas Nelson & Zondervan
1663 Liberty Drive
Bloomington, IN 47403
www.westbowpress.com
1 (866) 928-1240

Because of the dynamic nature of the Internet, any web addresses or links contained in this book may have changed since publication and may no longer be valid. The views expressed in this work are solely those of the author and do not necessarily reflect the views of the publisher, and the publisher hereby disclaims any responsibility for them.

Any people depicted in stock imagery provided by Thinkstock are models, and such images are being used for illustrative purposes only. Certain stock imagery © Thinkstock.

ISBN: 978-1-5127-3129-3 (sc)
ISBN: 978-1-5127-3128-6 (hc)
ISBN: 978-1-5127-3127-9 (e)

Library of Congress Control Number: 2016904162

Print information available on the last page.

WestBow Press rev. date: 3/9/2016

CONTENTS

Introduction	vii
Part 1: The Anchor Comes	1
Chapter 1: Adrift	3
Chapter 2: The Anchor on Earth	8
Part 2: The Anchor in You	23
Chapter 3: Anchored in Christ	25
Chapter 4: Abiding in the Vine	34
Chapter 5: Decide to Abide	43
Chapter 6: Bearing Fruit	55
Chapter 7: Spiritual Fruit	61
Part 3: Anchored to Love	79
Chapter 8: Anchored for a Purpose	81
Chapter 9: Anchored in the Storm	98
Chapter 10: Anchored in Hope	111
Conclusion	121

INTRODUCTION

Something about boats floating on peaceful water reaches deep into the soul; you know, those beautiful scenes of picturesque fishing boats lying at anchor on a calm, glassy bay, with not a hint of wind or a cloud in the sky.

But something about seeing boats tossed on a restless sea also stirs images and emotions: think of a fishing trawler inching its way toward a harbor through a raging storm. Tossed by waves and fierce winds, it strains to steer clear of rocky outcroppings while searching for a deep channel leading to calm waters.

There's quite a contrast between the two. The one pictures peace, tranquility, and safety, while the other portrays turbulence, anxiety, and danger. In this world, our souls so often long for the calm serenity of peaceful harbors, but it always seems as if we're surrounded by an ominous ocean. As Christians, we hear of a peace that passes understanding, but so often we find ourselves filled with worry and even downright despair.

Look around. Do you see people living selflessly and caring for others? The storehouses of the world's poverty-plagued masses filled? Genuine happiness in every home? Peace reigning over the earth? Multitudes leading secure, useful lives?

Nothing could be further from the truth. Everywhere is found sin and misery, war and disaster, pride and selfishness, starvation and greed—*and* harried humans striving for acceptance and a reason for living. Yet the world drifts along on a sea of false hopes and uncertainty. Sadly, many a Christian is drifting in the same boat.

I often hear people wonder, *What am I doing wrong? Why do I still have problems? How come I'm so unhappy?* So many wander aimlessly through life, grasping for fulfillment, groping in the darkness, and languishing in bondage to the ways of the world. Even sincere, seeking believers suffer feelings of insecurity and lack of purpose. Often, the answer to their plight lies in not knowing what God's definition of a meaningful life really is.

Like a boat, you must be anchored to something so sure, so solid, and so immovable you cannot be carried away when the violent storms of life rage around you. Even boats in peaceful harbors experience times of fierce winds, high waves, and torrential rains. But if their anchors are set firm, they can ride out the storms and emerge unscathed, ready to be useful vessels once more.

People may come to a saving knowledge of Jesus Christ as their Lord and Savior, but few realize the fullness of what Jesus saved them for. Since this world is a seething, stormy sea of uncertainty, how can anyone expect to navigate its reaches unless they are grounded on the words of the solid Rock?

Thankfully, there is an anchor for your soul, the incarnate God himself, Jesus Christ. His place as your secure mooring and your power for living above the uncertainty and storms will be our focus in this book, for then you can live a productive, fruit-bearing life for his glory and fulfill the purpose for which he created you.

In a world lost in sin and depravity, you must endure the winds of adversity. But instead of spelling disaster, such fierce gales can sweep in bountiful blessings. Your great God longs for you to experience the calm quiet waters of real, abundant life, even in the midst of troublesome times.

Jesus himself will teach and equip you to live a meaningful, fruit-filled existence. His own life will be your example. His death will be a reminder of your own. His resurrection will be your hope. His ascension will be your power. His presence will be "Christ in you, the hope of glory."[1]

---

[1] Col. 1:27. To make reading easier throughout the book, direct Scripture references are generally footnoted at the bottom of the page on which that reference occurs. The same is true for many indirect references as well.

PART 1

THE ANCHOR COMES

CHAPTER 1

ADRIFT

*"Take my life, and let it be
consecrated, Lord, to Thee."*[2]

We long to be loved and to be useful, and that's just what God wants for us. His entire universe was created out of love—a love we can hardly comprehend. Before humankind was created, the most glorious, loving relationship between God the Father and God the Son already existed. And out of this mutual, selfless, giving spirit came the motivation to create a people with whom to share that love, for God is love, and love gives.

Placing Jesus as the solid anchor in life's sea of uncertainty is the only way to fulfill the longing of your heart. God's love for you and all humankind cannot be understated, or you will miss Christ's teaching on life, love, power, and purpose. In fact, our Lord's position in your life is so important I need to first present the history behind it.

In the Image of God
In the beginning everything was good—the heavens and the earth, man and woman, plants and animals. Everything God created

---

[2] Havergal, Frances. "Take My Life and Let it Be." [last modified date] accessed June 1, 2015. https://www.hymnal.net/en/hymn/h/445.

through Jesus Christ was declared good by the Maker.[3] Surrounded by God's love and made in his image, humans set about being useful and praising the Creator for a love that radiates from his very essence.

Yet shortly after the world began, something terrible happened, changing all that was created good into something decaying, dying, and rotting: sin. Rejecting God's security and the significance they were given, Adam and Eve chose to embark on their own journey to self-fulfillment, one taken apart from God through acquiring knowledge he had forbidden.[4]

The resulting shame and confusion invaded God's peaceful realm of perfection. The guilty couple was judged, chastised, and banished from his presence, a fate they would pass down to their children and all their descendants to this very day. Without God as their anchor, they were set adrift in a world where death replaced life, fulfillment gave way to emptiness and despair, and love became distrust and hatred.[5]

However, God's love didn't change. Over time, and through chosen men and women, he showed his continuing interest in humans by rewarding faith in his unseen presence. Noah built an ark. Abraham and Sarah received a son. Moses led the Egyptians out of bondage. Later, God instituted plans for a tabernacle, and he came and dwelt there—still out of contact with all but the high priest, but nearer.

Afterward, Joshua led the Israelites, the people God chose to work through, into the Promised Land. Yet the Israelites chose to rebel and seek other gods, even in the very land God had promised and given. People did what was right in their own eyes, and in time God left their presence—again.

Hundreds of years later, the Roman Empire swept across the landscape, conquering every nation in sight, including Israel. Strong Jewish legalists, however, continued to rule the land in religious and civil matters, and the darkness never seemed deeper. God remained missing from the national scene.

---

[3] Gen. 1
[4] Gen. 3
[5] Gen. 3:23–4:16

Impossible as it may seem and in the face of continual rejection, God's love was poised to reach heights never dreamed of, except by prophetic voices that saw far into the future and foretold the coming of the greatest demonstration of love the world would ever witness.

The Fullness of Time
At just the right time—the "fullness of time"[6]—with the Promised Land in dark despair, the Promised One came onto the scene. The King of Kings first greeted his world in a stable nestled near the little town of Bethlehem. He was born to an outwardly normal couple from Nazareth, a city in the despised region of Galilee. However, no ordinary king was Jesus. He was *Immanuel*—God with us[7]—yet he grew up a carpenter's son, virtually unknown to anyone outside his hometown.

But when he reached age thirty, the age required in order to preach as a rabbi, Jesus set out to publish the good news that his Father was going to show his love for all people by forgiving their sins. Also, he proclaimed that he was ushering in another kingdom, a spiritual realm where peace and love reigned and would one day lead to an eternity of love in heaven.

Wherever Jesus went, he proved his relationship to his Father by healing the sick and raising the dead, although his kinship with God went unrecognized. Those deeds, along with the message of repentance he preached, drew the attention of not only the poor and downtrodden, but also that of Jewish leaders, the scribes and Pharisees. They especially became alarmed when Jesus elevated love for God and man above their traditions, and their concern turned to anger and hatred when he claimed to be the Son of God and equal with his Father.[8]

The final straw for these leaders was when Jesus raised a dead man to life. The news of this astonishing act quickly reached the ears of those in the nearby holy city of Jerusalem, prompting such

---

[6] Gal. 4:4
[7] Matt. 1:23
[8] John 10:30

an enthusiastic entrance for this godlike man to that city a few days later that the Jewish leaders then agreed he must be put to death.[9]

Having failed at earlier attempts to kill Jesus on their own, the Jews took him before Roman leadership for the crime of claiming to be a king. An agonizing Pilate sentenced him to be crucified—the form of death prescribed for a foreign criminal—after the Jews hurled accusations while Jesus stood silently by, refusing to defend himself. So, after carrying his own wooden cross to the top of a hill, spikes pierced his hands and feet, the cross was raised, and the King of love and life died.[10]

But death could not hold him, for on the third day following his crucifixion, he arose and appeared to astonished people on many occasions over many days. Finally, after being reunited with his disciples and sharing important and encouraging words with them, he ascended from their midst into heaven.

The good news of eternal life in Jesus rapidly spread. With his words echoing in their hearts and risking imprisonment and death, his followers trekked first to Jerusalem, then to Judea and later to Rome, North Africa, Spain, and eventually most of the known world. The apostle Thomas (a doubter no more after his aha moment upon meeting the risen Jesus, seeing his wounds, and exclaiming, "My Lord and my God!"[11]) brought this glorious message all the way to India.

But almost immediately, many gospels spread across the landscape that deviated from the indwelling presence of our Lord and our God as humankind's new, abundant life. Eventually, the inevitable apathy of an empty doctrine set in. Even before the beloved apostle John died, the Lord Jesus himself pronounced that the followers at Ephesus had left their first love.[12] And everywhere the fire of the good news went, the initial flame sooner or later grew dim. It doesn't take long for zeal to cool, and so it did. Jesus had largely turned into an institution.

---

[9] John 11
[10] John 18–19
[11] John 20:28
[12] Rev. 2:4

As time went on, the established church grew and became a mighty force, while persecution drove the true church underground. Furthermore, a subtle force began to grow, a spirit of the exaltation of man, which surfaced during the Renaissance. This spirit led to lives of self-centered thoughts and actions—in reality, no life at all—which has reached its greatest heights during this era of democracy. Today, in an age when self-government has swept around the world, self-fulfillment is perched on the thrones of its citizens.

Where Are You?
Do you feel loved? Useful? Is your life characterized by sacrificial giving? Are you oriented toward others? Is your heart overflowing with peace? Are you anchored, secure from the storms surrounding you? Or do you have an uneasy, restless feeling that something isn't right?

There really is acceptance, love, and purpose in life. The answer to all of life's critical questions lies in the following pages. The solution may surprise you. It definitely will challenge you. But if you believe, it will revolutionize your life.

CHAPTER 2

THE ANCHOR ON EARTH

"The Spirit of the Lord is upon Me, because He has anointed Me to preach the gospel to the poor. He has sent Me to heal the brokenhearted, to preach deliverance to the captives and recovery of sight to the blind, to set at liberty those who are oppressed."[13]

Jesus came to earth with the all-encompassing purpose of showing God's love to men and women, a love comprised of many facets. As Immanuel, his words carried the authority of heaven. In this chapter we will delve deeper into his revolutionary teaching to find out what this God-made-flesh Messiah offered his creation and what he expected of them as well.

The Lamb's Kingdom
One day, as Jesus strode down a dusty path leading to the banks of the Jordan River, John the Baptizer, his cousin, spied him approaching and uttered words that shook the heavens. "Behold!

---

[13] Luke 4:18 NKJV; cf. Isa. 61:1–3

The Lamb of God who takes away the sin of the world!"[14] Jesus thus stepped out of obscurity in Israel and into the public limelight.

On one occasion early in his ministry, the unrecognized King of Kings and Lord of Lords sat down on a mountainside in the position of a teacher and began teaching his disciples about a new kingdom, with a crowd of curious onlookers hanging on every word.[15] Citizens of this kingdom saw no hope in themselves, he said. Instead, they mourned over their sin and recognized their need to rely on God and his power; yet they would inherit the earth. They hungered and thirsted for a truly righteous life in the sight of God, and they would be filled.

Citizens of the kingdom were merciful to others out of hearts grateful for the mercy shown to them. They continually strove to be holy, and their motives were pure. They felt a strong desire to bring God's peace to their fellow humans. People in this realm encountered resistance from those without, but in the face of persecution they rejoiced, for they brought light and salt to a dark, confused world.

The most astonishing aspect of this kingdom's citizens was, perhaps, that even though they mourned, hungered, thirsted, and encountered persecution, they were *blessed*, "envied, and spiritually prosperous [with life-joy and satisfaction in God's favor and salvation, *regardless of their outward conditions*]."[16]

You can be sure that feeling happy about being persecuted was a new concept to these wondering ears. This new realm Jesus described was radically different from their idea of a Promised Land. Hundreds of years after an anointed deliverer was prophesied, a messiah, the land still waited for that someone with power to liberate the Israelites from Roman domination and reinstate a reign like Solomon's earlier years. However, such a life seemed only a dream, especially to the common people. Though everyone in the nation suffered under the rule of the Romans, the poorer class also suffered under their own religious leadership

---

[14] John 1:29 NKJV
[15] Read Matt. 5–7
[16] Matt. 5:7 AMP

and all the exacting laws and traditions added to Mosaic law over the years.

Jesus then astounded his listeners again by saying that though the law was expected to make people righteous, God required a life surpassing even what the law dictated. He gave his listeners a mental picture of a spiritual kingdom, one where people used righteous judgment and forgave each other, where they didn't worry about the future, and where their lives did not consist of storing up earthly possessions. Instead, they would find their hope and treasure in an unseen eternity in heaven.

He summed up his manifesto with this pronouncement: "In everything, do to others what you would have them do to you, for this sums up the Law and the Prophets." He then warned that both the road and the entrance gate to this eternal kingdom were narrow, that "ferocious wolves" would try to attack them along the way, and that people's motives would be recognized by their fruit.

As he concluded his revolutionary teaching, Jesus stated that those who put into practice what he said were building their houses on a rock, and they would stand through fierce rain and wind. However, those who heard his words and ignored them were building their houses on sand and would be washed away when the storms of life struck.

Traversing dusty, often rugged terrain, Jesus preached about a kingdom that was not *on* this earth, yet it was present among them and *in* them! The nations of the world would seek after the things of the world, but the true kingdom would be given to those who strove to enter it by living in love with Jesus and his Father. He even went so far as to say that its citizens must love their enemies.

While on earth, Jesus spoke of love, repentance, mercy, righteousness, and good deeds. Besides healing the sick and diseased, he showed compassion for widows and the poor. He carried himself with an appealing grace that reached out to untouchables, women, children—everyone—putting feet to his message. He manifested the attributes of God and commanded his followers to do likewise. Repeatedly, he used the phrase, "You have heard … *but I say* …," speaking with an authority not even the teachers of the law possessed.[17]

He Came to Show Us God
One of the most striking pronouncements from the prophets of the past was surely that this foretold Messiah was to be called *Immanuel,* meaning *God with us.*[18] As we read the accounts of our Lord's birth, we see a few were aware Jesus was destined to be that liberator. But for the rest, with the exception of a visit to the temple as a young boy, his future greatness was hidden. Centuries earlier, on the occasion of dedicating the temple, King Solomon had exclaimed, "But will God in very deed dwell with men on the earth? Behold, heaven and the heaven of heavens cannot contain thee!"[19] The answer to Solomon's question was yes; God would and did dwell with humankind: "He came unto his own."[20]

He came. Say those two words over and over. Do you feel their deep significance? Just think of what Jesus left behind when he was born: the constant communion of love with his Father; the perfection of heaven; the eternal kingly riches; and much more. Then contrast that perfect world and station of life with what he faced here at his birth: the lowliest birthplace; simple peasant parents; a life of simplicity and drudgery; and, in the future, hatred, rejection, and an early, agonizing death. Obviously, Jesus didn't think of himself when the time came to be born to a poor Jewish couple.

You and I and the rest of humanity were more important to him than being equal with God. That's how much he loved us! Even though he knew what it would take to buy us back, Jesus came to pay the terrible price of the sin of all humanity. He came to give us love and a purpose-filled life. He came to give *his* life in order to give *us* life throughout all eternity. Over the thousands of years of man's folly, God's love had never changed.

Jesus came in the exact likeness of his unseen Father. He said

---

[17] Matt. 5: 20–44
[18] Matt. 1:23
[19] 2 Chron. 6: 18
[20] John 1:11

those who saw him saw the Father.[21] To the Jews, who claimed Abraham as their father, Jesus made this astounding statement: "Before Abraham was born, I am" (the same name God had told Moses to use to identify God as the one who sent Moses to lead his people out of Egypt)![22] In other words, Jesus was stating, *I am the "I am" who was before Abraham, even though Abraham died two thousand years ago! I am*—the self-existing One.

Yet Jesus came from God as a man, having laid aside heavenly glory. He stated flatly, "The Son can do nothing by himself ... Whatever the Father does, the Son also does."[23] So as Jesus moved about, preaching and showing compassion by healing, the onlookers were actually seeing God in man at work. The Israelites witnessed God's love when Jesus raised people from the dead. They saw God's compassion when Jesus healed a woman who touched the hem of his garment. His disciples felt God's patience as Jesus dealt with their lack of understanding. Little children tasted God's gentleness as they sat on the knees of the Master. Jesus came to show humankind what God was really like.

But that was only the beginning. Let's look at other reasons for his coming.

He Came to Give Us Life

> In the beginning was the Word, and the Word was with God, and the Word was God ... *In him was life*; and the life was the light of men.[24]

> And this is the testimony: God has given us eternal life, *and this life is in his Son. He who has the Son has life;* he who does not have the Son of God does not have life.[25]

---

[21] John 14:9
[22] John 8:58 NIV
[23] John 5:19 NIV
[24] John 1:1, 4 (emphasis mine)
[25] 1 John 5:11–12 NIV (emphasis mine)

> I am the light of the world: he that followeth me shall not walk in darkness, but shall have *the light of life.*[26]

Jesus came into a dying world where men and women loved darkness instead of light because their deeds were evil. But he said he didn't come to condemn sinners: "God sent his only begotten Son into the world, that *we might live* through him."[27] Jesus, the light of life, came to save them. Indeed, he was life! "I am ... *the life.*" [28]

Eternal Life

> For as the Father hath life in himself; so hath he given to the Son *to have life in himself;*[29]

> The thief cometh not, but for to steal, and to kill, and to destroy: *I am come that they might have life,* and that they might have it more abundantly.[30]

> But these are written, that ye might believe that Jesus is the Christ, the Son of God; and that believing *ye might have life through his name.*[31]

The Bible clearly shows that Jesus was life and that he came to bring the life of God into the hearts of men. Those who believed what he said would have new hearts with new a purpose and a real love. However, Jesus made a definite distinction between temporal and eternal life. He said a man was to lay up treasure *in heaven* by working hard for the food that lasts unto *everlasting life,* not

---

[26] John 8:12 (emphasis mine)
[27] 1 John 4:9 (emphasis mine)
[28] John 14:6 (emphasis mine)
[29] John 5:26 (emphasis mine)
[30] John 10:10 (emphasis mine)
[31] John 20:31 (emphasis mine)

investing his life on the earth building bigger barns.[32] Though he spoke of his kingdom being near,[33] even within a person,[34] he made it clear his was not an earthly kingdom but one that was spiritually discerned—*a heavenly kingdom and* an eternal life going on and on after this world was gone.

Many of the miracles performed by our Lord pointed directly to everlasting life. The healing of a man born blind illustrated that Jesus, though he loved and cared for the sick and had great compassion for them, had a higher, heavenly purpose in mind.[35] These supernatural events would be talked about, written down, and passed on, so by believing the miracles all humankind might see him as the way, the truth, and the life and gain real life, both now and forever, through his name.[36]

No wonder Jesus stood out! He was real life in a world of death, decay, and despair. Jesus said, simply but assuredly, "I am the resurrection and the life."[37] In other words, *I raise the dead and give them life—eternal, true life.* He knew he was the only one who could give this true life without end: "No man cometh unto the Father, but by me."[38] As he prayed on one occasion to his Father, Jesus said, "This is life eternal, that they might know thee the only true God, and Jesus Christ, whom thou hast sent."[39]

Jesus also told his disciples that he lived in his Father and his Father in him, and if they also lived in him, he would give them that life. Living in Jesus and for Jesus, together with Jesus living in them and for them, would bring them heavenly life on earth, for Jesus was "the image of the invisible God,"[40] the source of life.

Jesus recounted other requirements for one who would inherit

---

[32] John 6:27; Matt. 3:2
[33] John 6:27; Matt. 3:2
[34] Luke 17:21
[35] John 9:1–40
[36] John 20:31
[37] John 11:25
[38] John 14:6
[39] John 17:3
[40] Col. 1:15

this eternal true life: one should 1) not lay up treasure for himself;[41] 2) have total, uncompromising devotion to him;[42] 3) do good;[43] 4) believe in him;[44] 5) partake of him;[45] and 6) abide in him.[46]

Jesus also taught that man would live by him[47]—his words were life[48]—and that he gave not only life, but *abundant* life.[49] He also preached that there would be not only a cost to man—giving up all to follow Jesus—but the unfathomable cost to Jesus himself: his own life.

Consider for a moment that out of the one hundred-plus times the word *life* in its various forms is used in Matthew, Mark, Luke, and John, fifty of them occur in the gospel of John. John's account, the most intimate of the four, reveals Jesus's thoughts concerning his role as the Son of God through the eyes of "the disciple whom Jesus loved."[50] From them, the importance placed by the Son on the kind of life offered by his Father becomes crystal clear. Those who loved their lives would lose them, but those who hated their lives in this world would keep them for life eternal.[51]

Through Jesus, all people might live because he would dwell in them by faith through his Spirit. The Lord Jesus—the Lamb of God who takes away the sin of the world—would give up his life for his sheep.[52] By his resurrection from the dead, he would break the power of death and sin. And because he still lived after death, those who believed in him would also live, both now and forever.

---

[41] Matt. 6:19–20
[42] Matt. 4:4; Luke 4:18
[43] Luke 10:30–37
[44] John 3:15-16; 11:25–26; 6:47
[45] John 6:51, 53, 54
[46] John 15:10
[47] John 5:25
[48] John 5:24
[49] John 10:10
[50] John 21:20; 13:23
[51] John 12:25
[52] John 10:11, 15, 17

He Came to Love

Remember this verse in Jeremiah, "I have loved thee with an everlasting love"?[53] That's God talking, and you can be sure his love never stops. Through the thousands of years between the garden of Eden and the baby of Bethlehem, and despite the turning away of his children to false gods, God loved the world. He loved it so much that he planned to give the dearest, most precious thing to him so he could be reunited with his creation. And that's why Jesus came. He taught that love was the way to true life. The Father loved his disciples, Jesus himself loved them, and his followers were to love each other.

Jesus once instructed a certain lawyer on this point, after this learned and esteemed man asked Jesus what one had to do to inherit eternal life. Jesus responded with a question of his own. He asked the scribe, well-versed in the law and traditions, for his opinion as to what the law said about inheriting eternal life. The lawyer responded and answered his own question—correctly—at the same time; one was to love God completely and also love his neighbor. Jesus then affirmed the reply saying, "This do, and thou shalt live."

Then Jesus told his listener of a Samaritan, one from a people hated by the Jews, who came to the aid of a Jew in distress and showed mercy after a Jewish priest and Levite had each passed by the unfortunate man, unmoved. When Jesus asked the lawyer who he thought was a true neighbor to the one in need, the man had to admit it was the Samaritan who showed love. Jesus responded, "Go, and do thou likewise."[54]

Jesus made the path to fellowship with him plain—love God, love one another. This was, perhaps, the preeminent requirement to the life Jesus gave, one that this particular lawyer and the rest of the religious hierarchy had probably never before considered. Their idea of life was bound to their traditions and the expectation of a political freedom wrought by a political messiah.

Our original parents had violated the one commandment

---

[53] Jer. 31: 3
[54] Luke 10:25–37

they were given, which had love for God and for each other bound up in it, and they were banished from God's presence. Perhaps you think God was really angry. After all, Adam and Eve were evicted from the garden, and a flaming sword blocked them from ever returning. Surely, only a vengeful God would do that!

But, in effect, they were spurning the Lord's love and robbing him of the glory he deserved for being such a loving Father. Did you ever think about the sadness that gripped the Father and Son in seeing the man and woman they created thumb their noses in God's face and go their own way? Yes, God was angry, and the relationship between God and his creation did change. But even so, God's eternal love remained the same.

Think about the prodigal son story Jesus told. The son left his father and his estate to go his own way, and over time, he ended up living a wretched life as a pauper. Yet the father's love toward him never changed. He was always waiting for the son to realize what he had done and to return; he was prepared at any moment to welcome him back and extend his love to the one who had done him wrong. God's love is like that.[55]

Jesus displayed a deep love for his disciples. Just before the last Passover meal they would share and less than twenty-four hours before his own human life ended, he gave them their last in-person life lesson. John sets the scene: "Having loved his own which were in the world, he loved them unto the end,"[56] and then he washed his disciples' feet as an example of servant love. Then followed the most profound discourse on love the world will ever hear. Here's a portion of it, and notice the prominence of love:

> A new commandment I give unto you, that ye love one another; as I have loved you, that ye also love one another. By this shall all men know that ye are my disciples, if ye have love one to another.[57]

---

[55] Luke 15:11–32
[56] John 13:1
[57] John 13:34–35

He that hath my commandments, and keepeth them, he it is that loveth me: and he that loveth me shall be loved of my Father, and I will love him, and will manifest myself to him ... If a man love me, he will keep my words: and my Father will love him, and we will come unto him, and make our abode with him. He that loveth me not keepeth not my sayings: and the word which ye hear is not mine, but the Father's which sent me.[58]

He Came So Man Would Believe
If love drove Jesus to earth to give love, believing in him drives man to abide in that love and give it to others. Jesus was emphatic about who he was and what man had to do in order to be in a right relationship with his Father. Since Jesus was the *Truth*[59] and the truth was in him,[60] the paramount issue was, according to the Master, believing what *the Truth* said.

John's gospel uses the various forms of the word *believe* almost ninety times, nearly the same number of occurrences as *life*. The apostle recorded sixty instances alone where Jesus himself used the word, since he knew the gift of genuine eternal life was of no benefit to his hearers unless they believed in the One who made the offer.

Jesus came so everyone would believe in him.[61] During his three years of public ministry, many did believe after seeing signs and wonders, but Jesus criticized those who would not believe unless he performed miracles.[62] He gave insight into the spiritual nature of his kingdom when he said to an inquiring Pharisee named Nicodemus, "If I have told you earthly things, and ye believe not, how shall ye believe, if I tell you of heavenly things?"[63]

---

[58] John 14:21, 23–24
[59] John 14:6
[60] Eph. 4:21
[61] John 1:7
[62] John 4:48
[63] John 3:12

Jesus went on to tell him that eternal life was there for those who believed him. On the other hand, those who didn't believe would not see life.

One day, a royal official who believed Jesus could heal his son, who was very sick, pleaded for the lad, and Jesus did what he asked. As a result, the official's entire household believed in Jesus as well.[64] Later on, Jesus healed a man on the Sabbath. Then the Jews began persecuting him and became determined to kill him when he called God his Father. Jesus responded by telling them his Father loved him dearly, and those who did not believe the Son did not honor the Father.[65]

Jesus made it absolutely clear that coming to him for life would be the only way a man could receive it and that the Scriptures backed him up:

> The works which the Father has given Me to finish—the very works that I do—bear witness of Me, that the Father has sent Me. And the Father himself, who sent Me, has testified of Me. You have neither heard His voice at any time, nor seen His form. But you do not have His word abiding in you, because *whom He sent, Him you do not believe. You search the Scriptures, for in them you think you have eternal life; and these are they which testify of Me. But you are not willing to come to Me that you may have life.*[66]

He Came to Abide
When God created the world, he did two things that would later find their eternal fulfillment in Jesus. First, he breathed into him the spirit of life. Afterward, he walked with the man (and later the woman as well) he had made, and together they had sweet fellowship.

---

[64] John 4:46-53
[65] John 5:1–23
[66] John 5:36–40 NKJV (emphasis mine)

So in order to remedy the disciples' sin-nature problem, Jesus surprised them yet again by saying the Holy Spirit would come to live in them, guide them into all truth, cause them to remember what Jesus had said, and give them the power to do even greater things than Jesus himself had done. In fact, Jesus said he would live in them.

Jesus knew that, without his continual presence, man would falter and fail to obey God's loving commands. So he flatly stated to those gathered around him that if he didn't die and go to the Father, his Spirit could not come and dwell in them. Further, without Jesus, they couldn't do anything.[67] All the wisdom and comfort he taught and talked about hinged on his presence.

Then the Lord Jesus painted a beautiful word picture to illustrate how his life would be transmitted to man: he would live in them *if* they dwelled in him. As grape branches draw life from the parent vine from which they emanate and grow, Jesus would impart his very life to them, and they would bring forth fruit. This was to be their purpose. But he warned them that barren branches would be pruned and possibly purged, because without his life-giving power, they would be unproductive. With him, however, they could even love each other as he had loved them.

He Came to Show Man God's Purpose

> "I seek not mine own will, but the will of the Father which hath sent me."[68]

What drove Jesus to do everything he did, including dying on a cross? What his Father wanted done was what he did. And what was that will that he so determinedly sought to fulfill? Everything Jesus did—putting aside his glory, seeking and saving the lost, showing them how to live and to love, how to be separate from the world, giving his life—encompassed God's will for Jesus.

God not only took on human flesh to pay the price of

---

[67] John 15:5 NKJV
[68] John 5:30

humankind's sin and give eternal life, he came to give humankind a purpose, an assignment for each one to complete, matching his own divine mandate from God.

> Behold, I say to you, lift up your eyes and look at the fields, for they are already white for harvest! And he who reaps receives wages, and gathers fruit for eternal life, that both he who sows and he who reaps may rejoice together.[69]

He Came to Give Us Hope
After humankind's fall, God intimated that one day Jesus would be victorious over Satan. Jesus did come as the Messiah to fulfill that hope, but by the time he was born, all hope had become centered on one who would free Israel from the Romans and restore it to its long-ago days of splendor. However, *hopeless* better describes the hearts of the people at that time. No one recognized that Jesus was indeed an even greater king than Solomon[70] and that the hope he offered rested on very different promises than those of an earthly conqueror.

Conclusion
Before the stars were set in place, Jesus already existed, was with God, and was God. As the full expression of God's thoughts, he became the author of the created world, and as the Light of the world, he came in the flesh to give the light of life to those who believed in him. To them he gave power to become the children of God. Jesus was the Word, the full testimony of God, full of grace and truth that he would later pour into those who believe.

Jesus was also the Lamb of God, who gave his life to take away the sin of the world, and he baptized in the Holy Spirit those who believed in him. He always contrasted the two spiritual kingdoms as darkness and light. Those who loved evil deeds loved the darkness. Those who practiced the truth and did what was

---
[69] John 4:35–36 NKJV; see also Matt. 28:19–20; Acts 1:8
[70] Matt. 12:42

right came to the light, showing their deeds were done by God in dependence on him.[71]

For a dying world, Jesus opened the way for humankind to come back into the Father's presence, which was true life. He told Nicodemus that he had to be born again into the life that God had intended.[72] The words he spoke were the truth, for he was the truth. Everything that belonged to God was in Jesus for all to see and hear. Speaking God's words and following his Father's will was his driving force: "My food is to do the will of Him who sent Me and to accomplish and completely finish His work."[73]

Jesus Christ worked continually to bring glory to the God of love. He did what the Father did because the Father loved him and showed him everything that he himself did. Miracles—referred to in John's gospel as signs—such as changing water into wine and healing a lame man demonstrated the inner power of God creating life out of death.

Our next theme gets personal. What Jesus said two thousand years ago is just as true and binding today. If you are to do today what Jesus said then, how does it all work? How does he become your anchor? If he lives in you, what's your part? We'll look deeper into those key terms Jesus was so emphatic about—*life, love, purpose, believing, abiding,* and *hope*—to find out how they can be transformed from interesting reading into life-changing action.

---

[71] John 3:19–21
[72] John 3:1–8
[73] John 4:34–38 AMP

PART 2

THE ANCHOR IN YOU

CHAPTER 3
ANCHORED IN CHRIST

He Lives in You

God created the world out of love, and love, by nature, must be shared. So in the beginning, God had a very intimate relationship with Adam and Eve, although a very brief one. But sin ruined that union and changed everything. For century after century humankind wandered, built cities, and made war. Then through Abraham, and because of the faith God knew he possessed, God eventually raised up the people with whom he would dwell.

For roughly two thousand years the Israelites, as they were called, had worshiped and followed God from afar, and what they knew of his ways was passed on by their priests and prophets. His *shekinah* glory dwelt in the tabernacle, but only the high priest was allowed to come before the Lord. Although nearer, God was still distant. Still, his intention was to dwell intimately with his people, just as he had in the beginning. And going back to God's original blueprint was the only way to get to where God intended man to be.

Then Jesus came to be the only sacrifice acceptable to his

Father in order to pay the price for humankind's sin. Even after the fellowship with humankind was shattered, Jesus came, this time as the way, the truth, and the life for helpless humanity. The path back to that lost paradise came through the cross—the death of the Son, of his love, Jesus. In so doing, Jesus became our all: our Alpha and Omega, the beginning, the end, and everything in between.

Who He Was and Is
God gave his Son the name above all names and stipulated that honor to him must come through honoring his Son: "This is My beloved Son. Hear Him!"[74] That pronouncement certified Christ's supremacy and became the key to understanding anything and everything about being anchored in Jesus. What the Son of God said—about his Father, his own life, and your life—had to be valued above all else. Never miss the unsurpassed importance of Jesus Christ in everything God planned.

In essence, Jesus said this about himself: *I am God's son, God in the flesh. Because I love you, I gave up my rightful place and came into this world to save you from your sins and give you real, everlasting life. I left the presence of my Father to give you the power to do my work after I go to heaven, just as I received power from my Father to do all you have seen me do. Through my Spirit I will live in you and give you life. I will teach you, give you strength, and set hope before you. Believe in me and keep on believing, for I alone am your anchor.*

But there was more to it. Jesus also came to reestablish that intimate relationship that was present in the beginning. You long to be loved and useful. That's good, because God sent Jesus to demonstrate just how much he loved you. He came to love you with an everlasting love, to give you the power of heaven, and to give you endless eternal happiness. He came to live in you, closer than you are to yourself. It was he who paid the price, opened the door, and provided the power for you to live a love-led, useful life.

---

[74] Luke 9:35 NKJV

Christ in You, the Hope of Glory
Here we are, travelers on this planet two thousand years beyond the ascension of Jesus into heaven and the coming of his Holy Spirit. True to his word, Jesus lives on in the hearts of those who believe.

In those who believe! Let this be clear: Jesus is life. He brought life and purpose to humankind, and his life and purpose must be in you. He said it, and you must honor what he says. Understanding what Scripture is telling you on this point is crucial: Jesus is the center of all things, and his is the voice of authority telling you how to live.

But Jesus has your best interests at heart. He pleads for you to believe, not as a demand but as an offer of a genuine life—his life, his purpose, his future. What he has said and continues to say carries the weight of eternity. You can believe what you want, but in the end you will be judged by your obedience to Jesus Christ. That's how important Jesus is.

Imagine a boat struggling through a raging sea toward a safe haven. But guarding the harbor's entrance is a treacherous shoal, one that has spelled doom to many a craft seeking safety. However, a lighthouse stands atop a cliff overlooking the dangerous waters. Its powerful beams cut like a knife through the darkness, warning of danger yet radiating a message of peace and comfort.

God sent Jesus as the light of life in order to show us his immense love, restore our fellowship with him, give us a purpose, and abide in our hearts to be our anchor. But you must believe that for it to be of value. Some may wonder, *Why do I need Jesus to be my indwelling anchor? I have all the light I need. I believe he died for me and is waiting for me in heaven. I thought that was all there was to it.*

Christ's own words show us that there is more. Let's see how his followers reacted to his message once he was crucified.

Believing and Life
On the night he was betrayed, Jesus put into motion the climax of the plan he and his Father had devised before the world was ever created. That evening he gave his disciples news that

must have pierced their hearts: he was leaving them. However, he softened the blow somewhat by saying that he was sending another comforter to live in them, teach them, and guide them. That comforter was to be the spirit of Jesus Christ himself.

And the next day he was crucified.

Deep sadness mixed with confusion filled the disciples after watching their beloved Master die an agonizing death that Friday. Stunned silence surrounded them. Why had he died? Something terrible had gone wrong. The love, peace, and wisdom they had grown to rely on seemed to have been buried with him—and now they were alone. Then on Sunday came inexplicable news: his tomb was found empty! What could it all mean?

Late that same day, fear turned to joy, confusion turned to reality, and sunshine replaced sorrow when Jesus suddenly materialized in the upper room where many followers had gathered. Later, after Jesus left and Thomas arrived, those who had been present when Jesus surprised them told Thomas the wonderful news. However, the doubtful disciple found their story impossible to accept, and the dear brother stated that he wouldn't believe without seeing the Lord *and* his wounds for himself. Imagine his shock and shame when, later on, Jesus did appear: "My Lord and my God,"[75] he exclaimed after seeing the Savior's scars.

The Master was gentle with Thomas despite the now-amazed disciple's demeanor, but he pointed to a crucial problem in Thomas's character needing immediate correction. He said, in effect, *Now you believe after you've had your visible proof. But Thomas, truly blessed will be the countless numbers who will not see me, yet believe.* Faith is the evidence of unseen things.

Immediately after John penned the conversation between Thomas and the Lord in his gospel account, he wrote this:

> Many other signs truly did Jesus in the presence of his disciples, which are not written in this book: But these are written, that ye might *believe* that Jesus is

---

[75] John 20:28

the Christ, the Son of God; and that *believing* ye might have *life* through his name.[76]

Believing is absolutely essential before real, genuine life can ever be imparted. Saints are called *believers* for a reason! The Holy Spirit guided John to write his gospel so that his readers down through the ages would believe and experience life, which is the fruit of believing. If you want to live a useful and purposeful life for Jesus, you must believe what he says—all of it. We've already seen how important life and believing were to Jesus and the New Testament authors. Now let's examine why believing is so crucial to being anchored in Christ.

Anchored in Belief
As the giver of life, Jesus knew every person would, of necessity, need to believe everything he said and stood for before he or she could die to his- or herself and put his or her life under his control. Coming down from the mountain where Peter, James, and John had heard God say, "This is my Son, whom I love … Listen to him,"[77] he had encountered a large crowd. A man stepped out of its midst and told Jesus that he had brought his demon-possessed son to be healed by Jesus's other disciples, but they had been unable to do anything. Jesus then said that they all were faithless, the disciples included.

When the father asked Jesus if he could do anything to help, Jesus responded with a question: *"What do you mean, 'if I can?' Anything is possible if a person believes."*[78] Then Jesus healed the lad.

The disciples then privately asked Jesus why they couldn't cast out the demon, and Jesus frankly told them that their unbelief had kept God's power from being released. He went further by saying that if they had a minute amount of belief as small as a tiny mustard seed, they could tell a mountain to move and it would.[79]

---

[76] John 20:30–31 (emphasis mine)
[77] Matt. 17:5 NIV
[78] Mark 9:23 NLT (emphasis mine)
[79] Matt. 17:20

You'll recall Jesus went to Bethany two days after hearing his dear friend, Lazarus, had died. Upon his arrival, Martha, Lazarus's sister, told Jesus that if he been there, her brother would still be alive. When he told her that her brother would rise again, she said she knew he would rise in the resurrection at the last day. Then Jesus confronted her with this amazing declaration: "*I am the resurrection and the life. He who believes in Me, though he may die, he shall live. And whoever lives and believes in Me shall never die. Do you believe this?*"[80]

Martha, no doubt confused, said she did believe. But when Jesus told the people to take away the stone covering the tomb, she protested, saying he that had been dead for four days and would be rotting. Once again Jesus challenged her, saying, "Did I not say to you that if you would believe you would see the glory of God?"[81] He had exposed Martha's lack of faith. Then he called, and a dead Lazarus rose to life and walked out.

Seeing Jesus
Jesus always blessed people for their belief in whom he claimed to be and what he could do. Let's see how that worked out for two troubled men over the time of the Lord's death and resurrection.

Jesus was very straightforward that night in the upper room. He knew what was happening nearby in the council of the Pharisees, and he knew where it would lead—to a garden in Gethsemane and on to a cross on Golgotha. Much of what he said had confused his disciples, and that wasn't all. The recent events—the Jewish leaders trying to capture him; Lazarus, dead for days, walking out of his tomb at Jesus's command; their Master's triumphal entry (or so it seemed) through the gates and the crowds into Jerusalem; and now this Passover meal itself—all spelled trouble. And they had yet to grasp the larger picture of who he was and what his intentions were, especially what he said about being lifted up and crucified.

Arguments had broken out during the meal. As the Lord

---
[80] John 11:25–26 NKJV (emphasis mine)
[81] John 11:40 NKJV

of heaven and earth stooped to wash the feet of his followers, pride reared its ugly head. Bickering broke out over who would be the greatest in the new kingdom. And one of the Twelve, exposed as a traitor, slipped from their presence into the night. Mysteriously, Jesus told them he too was leaving them after three trying, turbulent, and amazing years together. This after at least some, if not all, had pinned their hopes on him striding into Jerusalem as Messiah and setting everything in order. Instead, he had ridden in on a donkey. And now …

The Master's words no doubt pierced these troubled men's hearts when he told them to love each other as he had loved them, especially with their own words and acts of discord that night still ringing in their ears.

Jesus had implied that these faithful ones, who had stood with him for so long and through so much, would falter and fail in their attempt to make good Peter's boast that he would never deny his Lord. "Without me, you can do nothing,"[82] he flatly stated, summing up his assessment of how well they could love each other and spread the gospel on their own. Yet he also said that he was leaving to go to his Father. If that happened, how were they supposed to fulfill his command to preach the good news without him to lead them?

Perhaps the strangest words to their ears were those Jesus spoke of the Holy Spirit living inside them, that Jesus himself was coming to make their hearts his dwelling place—in each one of them! Strange tidings indeed …

On that resurrection morning, after what Jesus had said about being crucified came to pass, two very sad and confused disciples (though not of the original twelve) trod the road from Jerusalem to Emmaus, reliving the bizarre events of the past few days: the triumphal entry of Jesus into the city; that last meal with the Twelve and all that transpired there; the trek to the garden; the sudden appearance of the high priest's henchmen; Jesus dragged off first to the high priest, then to Pilate, and on to Herod. There was the rabid crowd of Pharisees and priests screaming for his

---
[82] John 15:5

crucifixion, the cross on his back, the agonizing march to the hill, the Messiah nailed to the cross. And death, the tomb, the guards. Then, that very morning, the astonishing report that the tomb was empty, and the Lord's body gone.

As the two, downtrodden and disheartened, tried in vain to make some sense of it all, they became aware of someone walking with them. The stranger spoke, asking what they were talking about, so they told him. After a bit and quite unexpectedly, the man began to chastise them for their lack of faith: "O fools, and slow of heart to believe all that the prophets have spoken; Ought not Christ to have suffered these things, and to enter into his glory?"[83]

So Jesus—for it was he who walked unrecognized with them—showed these tired travelers how the Scriptures had laid out God's grand plan to rescue sinful man from his doomed destiny of an eternity apart from God. They must have felt something stirring within as he spoke, for as they neared their destination and saw that the still-unrecognized Jesus appeared ready to continue on, they urged him to stay. All three entered a house, and upon sitting down Jesus took bread and blessed it and gave it to the wondering seekers. Suddenly, as if walking out of a fog onto a sunny mountain peak, their eyes were opened in recognition—they saw Jesus sitting before them. Then he vanished.

They turned to each other in wide-eyed amazement and exclaimed, "Did not our heart burn within us while He talked with us on the road, and while He opened the Scriptures to us?"[84]

That's the way it is with those who are sincerely seeking the truth. Even though slow to believe, Jesus continually confronts such people on the road of life and questions them about their faith. His Spirit leads to the truths he spoke regarding who he is and what God has planned for their redemption and new life. He proves that the power for such an adventure comes only from his indwelling presence in their hearts, leading them to burn inside with a longing to crucify any and every sinful desire and follow him.

---

[83] Luke 24:25–26
[84] Luke 24:32 NKJV

Jesus and Our Journey Ahead

It's sad seeing so many people today walking down a similar road. All they know of Jesus is his death on the cross, his body being placed in a grave, rising from the dead, and ascending into heaven. They have no joy of experiencing the risen Savior living and working in and through them. They hear news of an abiding Christ, but they are slow to believe. Someone else may have experienced the security and purpose of a life God had planned before creation, but not them.

But Jesus did not come simply to live a life that would serve as an example for humankind and then go off to heaven to be with his Father and wait for them. He didn't expect the two heading back to Emmaus to go back to the life they had lived before they met him. He wanted to become their inner guide through every step of their lives and take them on the adventure of a lifetime, always there to work out everything they would need for the journey ahead.

In the same way that Jesus challenged Martha, he poses two questions to each of us: *I say that I will give you peace and rest. I will be your light and your life. I will comfort you and give you strength. I will be your shepherd. I will give you a purpose. Do you believe what I say? Are you ready to put your life on the line to prove it?*

Imagine the beauty of a transformed life, one bringing the love of Jesus into every situation you face. Do you believe that Jesus can help you? Do you want to see and experience God's glory in your life? The only thing keeping it from happening is not believing that he lives inside you to make it happen.

Dear friends, Jesus is waiting to be your anchor in the confusion of life. He longs to open your eyes and for you to see him as God's central theme in history. He'll take you through Scripture and show his centrality in everything God did from Creation to this very moment. Read on and see how.

CHAPTER 4
ABIDING IN THE VINE

I am the true vine, and my Father is the husbandman. Every branch in me that beareth not fruit he taketh away: and every branch that beareth fruit, he purgeth it, that it may bring forth more fruit … Abide in me, and I in you. As the branch cannot bear fruit of itself, except it abide in the vine; no more can ye, except ye abide in me. I am the vine, ye are the branches. He that abideth in me, and I in him, the same bringeth forth much fruit; for without me ye can do nothing.[85]

For I know that nothing good dwells within me, that is, in my flesh. I can will what is right, but I cannot perform it. [I have the intention and urge to do what is right, but no power to carry it out.][86]

The world of Peter, John, James, Thomas, and the other disciples had turned upside down in three short years. Jesus

---
[85] John 15:1–2, 4–5
[86] Rom. 7:18 AMP

had taken the Law, to which they had faithfully adhered, and condensed it to loving God and loving others.[87] He had, in fact, quietly yet forcefully proclaimed that he embodied all that the Law required.[88] By his own holiness founded on love, he had shown them how far short they fell from being anchored in God.

An anchor keeps a boat steady and in place regardless of the conditions. But the disciples had proven beyond any doubt at the last supper with their Master that they were anything but firm and unwavering in their belief in him. Though in almost continual contact with Jesus, they were still mortal men who had tried to handle every encounter of life the only way they knew how—on their own. Without daily drinking from living waters, they would be helpless to bear fruit fit for a heavenly King.

Bible scholars call the last year of our Lord's life the "year of opposition," and for good reason. Early in his ministry, Jesus had pronounced that persecution awaited those who followed his good news of love and self-denial instead of the law based on the commandments of men. The Jews hated him from then on and eventually began plotting to kill him.

Although his disciples had learned much, the full understanding of the depth of humankind's sinful nature had eluded them. They couldn't see that although a person's spirit might be willing, the flesh was definitely weak. And they were also blind to their Master's deity, the fact that it was God in the flesh with whom they walked the dusty paths.

The Upper Room
Sadness *could* have filled the Savior's heart that evening as he and his disciples ate the last Passover meal that they would share. He knew he was going to die at only thirty-three years of age and that the gospel of God's love had been embraced by so few. If he died, what would happen to the few? But instead of acting

---
[87] Matt. 22:37–40
[88] Matt. 5:17

downhearted, he had confidently declared, "I have earnestly and intensely desired to eat this Passover with you before I suffer."[89]

In the face of all the opposition, hatred, and ignorance, why would Jesus have been so eager when he knew his betrayer would soon eat with him at the same table? The answer is love. He loved these men and all humankind, and this would be his last chance to demonstrate how much he cared through what he taught, encouraged, and exhorted. Let's revisit those crucial moments again to see exactly what was in our Savior's heart and how very critical his words are to experience him as your anchor. I urge you to reread John 13–17 to become familiar with the background of what follows.

Early on that evening, Jesus gave them one example of what love looked like by washing their feet. If they were puzzled as to why he, their Master, would stoop so low as to serve them, they were no doubt stunned when he said, "I am the way, the truth, and the life: no man cometh unto the Father, but by me ... *He that hath seen me hath seen the Father* ... Believe me that I am in the Father, and the Father in me."[90]

Jesus knew he would soon be the Passover lamb, the reality of what God had foreshadowed more than two thousand years earlier when he saved those Israelites who had wiped the blood of a spotless lamb on the doorposts of their homes in Egypt. Because of his upcoming crucifixion, his own blood would cover the sins of all men, including the ones gathered together with him, and would appease God's righteous judgment.

He also knew he was the lamb who would take away humankind's sin and restore our ability to walk with God. As the Word of God—God's testimony—made as a man, he knew the plan he and his Father had put into action, beginning with his miraculous birth, the event that brought peace on earth. Simply put, he became God in man, and soon his death, resurrection, and ascension would close the brief time in which he had moved among his children. So on his last night on earth, Jesus had a

---

[89] Luke 22:15 AMP
[90] John 14:6, 9, 11 (emphasis mine)

burning desire to prepare his disciples for the task of being his vessels to carry the good news wherever he would send them.

Jesus had told his bewildered followers that they couldn't do anything without him, thus exposing their total lack of ability to please God on their own. And Peter had proved him right when Jesus brought to the surface an "I know better than you" pride in the obstinate disciple.

In addition, an argument had arisen among the group as to who among them was considered the greatest—and this after their Lord and Master had washed their feet! Finally, while Jesus was later being questioned by the high priest, as a sad finale to the disciples' portrayal of self-centeredness, Peter would deny he even knew Jesus.

Before leaving the upper room, Jesus had revealed the climax of God's glorious plan. Through the comforter God would send, both Jesus and God the Father would live in those who believed; they would actually be inhabited by the God of eternity. These weak, helpless mortals could then lead victorious, useful lives, not by their own power but by the strength of the crucified, risen Lord himself flowing through them to the rest of the needy world.

Jesus had assured them that because he lived, they also would live, even though he was to be crucified the next day. Little did the disciples know that by doing so he would conquer death and rise from the dead, offering the gift of life he had won to everyone.

Abide in Me
Then came the moment when the spotless Lamb of God who takes away the sin of the world uttered these glorious words, "Dwell [abide] in Me, and I will dwell in you."[91] If they loved him and believed he loved them, the door to constant fellowship with their Savior would swing open.

Jesus was saying that if these eleven ordinary men who had been with him so long obeyed his command to love one another, he, the Father, and the Holy Spirit would all make their abode in them. He was declaring that the God of heaven and earth would

---
[91] John 15:4 AMP

make his home—literally "move in"—not in a tabernacle behind a curtain, but in the heart of each person who gave up his or her life and followed God's Son, Jesus Christ . They would become God's sons and daughters.[92]

The disciples' Master would then become their anchor, a solid, stabilizing, ever present, and consistently dependable foundation, and he would give them power to successfully face everything he faced and overcame in order to bring the gospel of his love to humankind. He had said before, "He who endures to the end will be saved,"[93] and because he would be in them to work his power in the midst of their weakness, such a life would now be possible.

Time had flown by. The group reclining around the low table had listened to the truth from the lips of God incarnate for perhaps hours. It's possible they may even have already left the upper room after the Passover meal and wound their way toward the nearby Mount of Olives and the tranquil peace of the garden of Gethsemane lying at its base as Jesus revealed his heart while he walked. He had told them of his love for them and told them to love each other in the same sacrificial way. Being weak mortals and prone to wander, abiding in him was the only way to live a life of victory over sin and death and fulfill God's purpose for their future, for such a life would produce fruit and result in true joy.

When the last precious grains of sand had made their way down the hourglass of Jesus's mortal life, he was just about to pray to his Father for these men who had stayed close to him to be one. But he had one last thing to share with them. After they finally affirmed their belief that he came from God, Jesus gave them this warning, and I paraphrase: *You say you believe, but in a short while you will all desert me and run away. In me alone you will find peace. You will experience tribulation and trials and distress and frustration in the world. But take courage: I have overcome it!*[94]

Eleven tired men, lost in a sea of confusion, arrived with their Master that night at the same garden where Jesus had gone

---

[92] John 1:12
[93] Matthew 24:13 AMP
[94] John 16:31–33

before to pray. What was going through their minds? The washing of their feet? Judas's sudden departure? The command to love? The clarity of Jesus's simple yet profound statement that he was returning to his Father? Had they remembered the times when Jesus stated he was to be lifted up so he could draw all men to himself? What about abiding in him? Jesus, the Father, the Holy Spirit all living in them?

Whatever they were thinking was soon overtaken by fitful sleep, while their Lord talked with his Father. And then, suddenly, the turmoil Jesus had predicted only a short while earlier erupted all around them. A crowd sent by the chief priests and elders arrested Jesus, and his disciples all did what Jesus had predicted: they fled.

Jesus knew what was in a man and, try as they might, his friends could not overcome the temptation to sin; they could not carry out their intention of doing what was right. True believing, Jesus knew, was not merely a mental agreement that he was the Son of God, but it also released his mighty power to love and do good deeds. However, that would take each one of them going through a crucifixion experience to accomplish.

Vines and Branches
If you knew you were going to die within the next twenty-four hours, and you had the chance to talk with those who were dearest to you, what would you say? Most likely you would share the things dearest to your heart, which is just what Jesus did with his disciples that pivotal evening. He spoke of love—love for his Father, for the disciples themselves, and for the world. Knowing he was about to suffer the death of a criminal and a foreigner, Jesus drew them deeper into his reason for coming so his disciples would remember his words and have a road map for their future without his physical presence. And he assured them that because he was sending the Holy Spirit to teach and guide them, they would be able to continue his legacy of sacrificial love.

In John's account of what occurred during the Last Supper, Jesus spoke some of the most important concepts you will ever read or hear. John opened his gospel with the wondrous news that God came to dwell with man. But on that Passover night, Jesus, the Word made flesh, built on his grand theme of spreading the good news he had proclaimed throughout his ministry by using the allegory, or parable, of a vineyard as an example of what this abiding in him would accomplish. He was the vine, and his disciples were the vine's branches. The purpose of a grape vine is to produce grapes. So in order for Christ's disciples to carry on his work, they had to be the channels through which his fruit was to be produced. They were to bear much fruit.

Pruning for Production
Producing high-quality grapes calls for the hands of a master gardener; the vines can't be simply left to themselves. In our Lord's example his Father was just such a gardener, one who would cut away barren branches in order for the remaining fruitful ones to carry more and better fruit. The point at which Jesus was driving was that his disciples should remain in him, just as surely as good branches remain in the vine, so his life-giving spiritual nutrients would continually flow from him to them—and through them.

Have you ever seen a productive grapevine? Usually in the early spring, the gardener prepares his vines for the growing season. But the sight greeting his eyes when he first beholds them is not a pretty one. All the leaves have fallen to the ground, and the branches droop bare and brown. But the gardener does not despair, for he knows the plants have been dormant and are awaiting the master's touch to renew them to productivity. With an expert's eye, he begins the pruning process. He concentrates on cutting away branches that are either dead or too far from the vine to be productive. Then the plant is ready to produce luscious, healthy fruit.

Jesus gave his disciples the key to being a productive branch—abide in the vine. To abide means to stay in a certain place. In the *King James Version*, the Greek word for *abide* is sometimes rendered *dwell, remain, continue,* or *endure*. Can you see what Jesus was getting at? He was saying, *Remain in me. Stay in me. Continue with me. Live in me and I will live in you.*

The vine is the support of the branch and source of all the nutrients necessary for producing fruit. Can a branch bring forth delicious grapes without drawing life-giving nutrition from the vine? Of course not. And just as the branch could not yield fruit without the vine, the disciples, soon to be left without the physical presence of their Lord, would be powerless to produce the fruit of the Spirit without being connected to the only One who could generate that fruit.

Rest in His Love
It was after Judas stole into the night to betray Jesus that our Lord gave the "new commandment"—"*Love* one another as I have loved you."[95] These words were all the more remarkable considering the horrible deed of satanic hatred Judas was enacting at that moment not far away and the self-centered actions of the others. Selfless love was the grand theme of God's relationship with man, so Jesus underscored its humble, sacrificial nature that evening. Look at the following references from John 13 and 14 and see how love dominated Jesus's last words of exhortation:

> He [Jesus] *loved* them [his disciples] unto the end.[96]
>
> A new commandment I give unto you, that ye *love* one another; as I have *loved* you, that ye also love one another. By this shall all men know that ye are my disciples, if ye have *love* one to another.[97]
>
> He that hath my commandments, and keepeth them, he it is that *loveth* me: and he that *loveth* me shall be *loved* of my Father, and I will *love* him, and will manifest myself to him ... If a man *love* me, he will keep my words: and my Father will *love* him, and we will come unto him, and make our abode

---
[95] John 13:34 (emphasis mine)
[96] John 13:1 (emphasis mine)
[97] John 13:34–35 (emphasis mine)

with him. He that *loveth* me not keepeth not my sayings.[98]

Only through constantly abiding in him in love—and him loving in you—can you hope to live a life of continual peace and purpose. In the next chapter, you will see how these precious words apply to your life.

---

[98] John 14:21, 23–24 (emphasis mine)

CHAPTER FIVE

DECIDE TO ABIDE

Deciding to abide in Jesus is actually pretty straightforward. Pursuing him as your anchor is a command, so as with all commands, you must choose his offer of abiding rest if you are to experience peace that passes understanding and usefulness in his kingdom.[99]

Maybe you feel you don't know Jesus much better than the Israelites knew God Almighty. Do you feel ill-prepared or too weak to live an abiding life? If you answer yes, that's okay because your humble admission is God's first requirement for working his wonders in you. Only the weak qualify for an abiding life in Jesus. Remember, the blessed are the poor in spirit, the mourners, those who hunger and thirst for righteousness. It is precisely those who recognize their weaknesses who are the ripe candidates to be filled with his abiding presence. Jesus cannot be yoked with someone who feels self-sufficient, for such people will not be prepared to move in concert with their Master when they yearn to go in a different direction.

When Jesus saved you, he never intended for you to work out your Christian experience on your own. He knows you can only

---

[99] John 5:19–27

gain the understanding and strength you need to do the will of God by leaning on his abiding presence.

Live in the Vine
Words cannot express just how much this amazing gift of Christ's abiding presence means. Think on this for a moment: What earthly king would ever offer to spend one night in the same house as one of his subjects? Yet Jesus—Immanuel, your Creator, your King—longs to show his love for you so much that he wants to make *you* his dwelling, the place where he remains. And more than this, he wants you to experience the fullness of his presence by being his vessel to bring love to the world. This is *God* who has promised to live in you, and his promises are sure. You can move through life with confidence when you live with the King.

Fruit always figured prominently in Jesus's teaching to illustrate his great love offered full and free to reclaim the lives of lost sinners. After his resurrection, he commanded his disciples to go into the entire world and share the good news of his love;[100] for believing this message would open the door for countless others to see and abide in Jesus as well. In his eternal wisdom, God uses transformed sinners who love each other to show his love to the lost. Therefore, our task is to display the fruit of the indwelling Christ so that the world can see his love.

Branches bear fruit; this you must not forget, or the principle of abiding means little. The branches are dear to the vine, for the vine needs healthy branches to produce fruit. It is in this context that Jesus issued the warning that without him, you can do nothing. In other words, he states, *If you are not abiding in me, consciously aware of my presence and in fellowship with me, you are helpless to bear fruit for my glory.*

Does that strike you as being a strong statement? It should, for this "impossible" task lies at the heart of who Jesus is and what God originally set out to accomplish by creating man. He brought into existence a people created in his image to love each other and to love him.

---

[100] Matt. 28:18–20; cf. Acts 1:8

Knowing the Vine
Abiding in Jesus means your faith in him is continuous, which makes sense. It's foolish to move in and out of a house. In the last chapter, we saw believing in who Jesus is and what he says is essential to always working under his power. Since you walk by faith and not by sight, you can't make any real progress in your knowledge of Jesus and usefulness to his kingdom unless you continually believe. Andrew Murray puts it this way:

> A soul filled with large thoughts of the vine will be a strong branch and will abide confidently in him. Be much occupied with Jesus, and believe much in him as the true vine. Say to Jesus, "I do believe you are living in me. I do believe you love me and want to love others through me. Please give me opportunities to share your love with others." Then believe that in his way and in his time he will give you what you ask for ... Do not fear that Jesus will not answer or that you are not worthy of such a privilege. *Remember, it is in the weak that Jesus can be strong.*[101]

Believe in Him as the True Vine
All the blessings and promises Jesus offers are yours when you abide in the true vine. You may begin your Christian walk with a heart to learn more of Jesus and grow in him, but since your faith is new and weak, you have much to learn about his love. Then, one day, you consecrate yourself to trust him with everything, and as you make your residence with him, your relationship changes. But you still may falter and slip back and lose valuable ground because you have made the mistake of thinking your abiding in Jesus was conditioned on a one-time decision. In reality it is a day-by-day and moment-by-moment experience. Never forget this: you are weak all the time, but he is strong—*all the time.*

---

[101] Andrew Murray, *Abide in Christ.* Springdale (PA: Whitaker House, 1979). [italics mine]

You may have fallen into the trap of abiding in yourself. Instead of trusting in Jesus, you trust in your own abilities and desires. You may embrace a certain teaching or philosophy, but in the end, it is you making the decisions.

Abide in the Good Shepherd's Arms
Have you ever seen sheep grazing in a grassy field? Jesus had much to say about these placid creatures, and looking at their ways will help us to understand the principle of abiding in him in a deeper way.

Sheep are raised in various locations all over the world. In England's southwestern "boot" along the coasts of Devon for instance, the climate is mild and the grass grows green and luxurious—a good place to be if you are a sheep. However, this portion of the country sits on a high plateau bordered by cliffs towering above the sea.

If you've been around sheep for any length of time, your observations have probably dispelled the preconceived notion you may have grown up with that sheep are simply docile, snowy white animals that peacefully munch on grass all day. It's a shock for most people to learn these "cuddly creatures" are often filthy, prone to disease, stubborn, easily frightened, not extremely intelligent, and wander wherever their stomachs lead. They require continuous oversight if the shepherd is to raise them to be contented, healthy, and productive animals. Left to their own, they will in time fall prey to parasites, predators, or their own gluttony or foolishness.

Now take an animal that loves to eat and wander, is stubborn and not very smart, and place it in a field next to England's craggy cliffs with grassy outcroppings dotting their fissures, and what do you get? Sheep in trouble! As the sheep follow their appetite, they seem unaware that narrow trails often lead to dead-end bluffs, a drop-off, and certain death on rocks below. A sheep grazing on the edge of the field while seeking the proverbial greener grass may find itself in peril simply because it follows its senses rather than its sense!

It's no wonder so many Bible passages compare people to

sheep, such as "All we like sheep have gone astray; we have turned every one to his own way."[102] And there's the parable of the lost sheep and the seeking shepherd.[103] Ever since the beginning of time, God has warned man of the dire dangers always close at hand, yet his danger signals so often go unheeded. "Prone to wander, Lord, I feel it," goes a line from a famous old hymn.[104] We wander off to what our flesh sees as the world's greener pastures, leaving our Shepherd behind.

Thankfully, the Lord Jesus, the good Shepherd, has invested his life in his creation and can be a personal shepherd to each sheep who puts its trust in him. Think on that: the good Shepherd, the one who gave his life for the sheep, makes his home in the hearts of those who choose to make their home in him.

Yes, we have a choice to make. Unlike the shepherd who physically restrains an ignorant animal, Jesus wants you to glorify his Father by choosing to listen to his voice and follow him on the path of righteousness. Your Shepherd speaks to you through his Holy Spirit, continually encouraging, exhorting, and chastising you to stay in the safety of his green pastures of love, away from the dangerous cliffs and stagnant pools of life that may lead to your destruction. He keeps you in his fold of usefulness instead of feeding on your own appetite. Under his care, you learn to help lead others into the fold where they too can live safely and find purpose. The rewards of following your Shepherd far outweigh the pleasure of feeding on your lusts. You simply have to choose his ways.

If you truly believe Jesus lives in you full-time to guide and empower you to live a holy, purposeful life, then take the next step and continually abide in the safety of his loving arms. Beginning your Christian experience was a momentous act in your life. You were new to the faith then, and the cares of the world had momentarily moved behind you. But adversity never

---

[102] Isa. 53:6
[103] Matt. 18:12–14
[104] Robert Robinson, "Come, Thou Fount of Every Blessing," *http://www.hymnsite.com/lyrics/umh400.sht* (June 1, 2015).

goes away. Even though welcome lulls may come, storms continue to appear on everyone's horizon. It is then that the reason for Christ's emphasis on dying to oneself and believing him begins to make sense.

At each critical moment, trusting in his call to not only believe but to abide in him becomes paramount; for what good will come from believing Jesus can work his wonders in and through you if you are not connected to his indwelling presence by the strong cord of faith? Before you are swallowed up by the waves of life, grab hold of your anchor.

Accepted and Abiding

Do you feel accepted by your beloved?[105] You must if you are to successfully abide in Jesus. Feel the love of Christ and believe that he accepts you regardless of your past, just as he accepted Paul, who had previously persecuted the Lord through his persecution of the saints. Since everyone has sinned and fallen short of God's glory, we are all in the same boat. Without exception, everyone to whom God extends his love has had a checkered past. All of us are weak, no matter how strong our fleshly determination and conviction. You may be the chief of sinners, as Paul humbly stated,[106] but God's love waits to entirely enfold you and use you in his kingdom, just the same.

You're in for a long and bumpy ride until you yield to the fullness of God's grace since what you do for the Lord will be done out of your own strength. In other words, you are attempting to work out your own righteousness by doing good works in order to gain acceptance. Make no mistake; good works *are* an essential component of God's purpose for us. Look at the mention of good works in the New Testament and their place of importance. Over and over again, through the mouth of Jesus, as well as others, we are commanded to do good deeds. Here are just two of those instances:

---

[105] Song 6:3
[106] 1 Tim. 1:15

> Let your light so shine before men, that they may see your good works, and glorify your Father which is in heaven.[107]

> For we are his workmanship, created in Christ Jesus unto good works, which God hath before ordained that we should walk in them.[108]

What is the difference between acceptable good works and those that aren't? It all centers on who does them. Is it you trying to gain acceptance, or Jesus inside you both prompting and empowering you to do good deeds? All the work you could ever do on your own will never fill the void of needing to be accepted. Only by believing in Jesus as your anchor will you ever find peace, power, and purpose in life. Remember, it is God in you who wills and acts according to his good pleasure.[109]

Peace in Abiding
One of the benefits of being a fruit-laden, abiding branch is the peace that comes with it. The comfort of a good home brings rest. Even the most basic dwelling can be a shining light that radiates warmth if made into a true home by the love of its inhabitants. If Jesus is our anchor, being at home with him brings peace, even amid the storms of life.

Have you ever been in a boat out on a lake when a storm came up? Most people assume being on an ocean in rough seas is far worse, yet large lakes such as Lake Superior also claim lives every year during stormy weather. The Sea of Galilee in Israel is 155 times smaller than Lake Erie, the smallest of the Great Lakes, yet tempestuous winds flowing down from the adjacent mountains can create huge waves, putting the tiny fishing vessels that ply its relatively shallow waters in extreme danger.

Such was the case one day long ago when Jesus and his disciples

---

[107] Matt. 5:16
[108] Eph. 2:10
[109] Phil. 2:13

set out to cross that sea. But a violent storm arose, creating waves so high that their craft was nearly swamped. The men became terrified—all, that is, except Jesus, who slept in the stern! When they awoke him, he spoke to the elements, "Peace, be still!"[110] The wind quit blowing. The waves subsided. And there was calm.

When the storm struck, the travelers with Jesus were certainly ignorant about him, for they had no idea who he really was. If they had, they would have known the turbulent waters were under his authority, regardless of whether or not he was asleep. The seas of life also present a formidable obstacle, yet the waters themselves are not the only hazard. Every mariner who has sailed life's ocean warns of reefs that may quickly appear and then vanish. Two of the most dangerous of these hidden dangers are fear and ignorance.

The disciples in the boat were more than just afraid—they were terrified and in a state of panic. Jesus pointed out that a lack of faith was behind their fear, as it always is. Therefore, it was impossible for them to experience calmness and serenity even though the Prince of Peace and the ruler of the elements was abiding in the boat with them through it all!

Without faith, the most pleasant, peaceful valley can instantly become a battleground. But secure in the abiding presence of Jesus, every conflict can be faced with inner serenity. Remember, Jesus is always in your boat, and you are secure as long as you are in touch with him.

What a wonderful invitation Jesus gives us when he says, "Come unto me, and I will give you rest,"[111] and what assurance we feel when he promises, "My peace I give unto you."[112] Even more, he gives us the blessed offer, "Learn from me."[113] So learn to abide. Coming to him is a privilege no one deserves yet everyone longs for, and the invitation to make your relationship with him deep and lasting is more wonderful still.

---

[110] Mark 4:39
[111] Matt. 11:28
[112] John 14:27
[113] Matt. 11:29 NIV

Trouble in Paradise
However, so many who have come to Jesus have not learned to abide in the rest he offers. That is sad because your anchor offers seekers a rest in his love from the anxieties and fears that surround us. Don't fear: Jesus is meek and lowly in heart, not a stern taskmaster. Although he experienced an environment of stress, he always walked on earth with the calm assurance that the love relationship between him and his Father would never be broken.

At this point you may be asking, *Well, I can see that abiding in Christ, the way you describe it, is going to mean a radical change in my life.* Have you come to the point where you are wondering, *Why am I here?* In the very first chapter I mentioned that most Christians feel a vague uneasiness about their lives. They sense that something is missing, yet they cannot put their finger on it. So many people are dissatisfied with the pace of life and the apparent lack of anything meaningful. There is frustration over being unable to meet all the demands life brings. Joy, peace, and rest elude them.

Do you long for a deeper experience with Jesus, an anchor for your soul? If so, the Holy Spirit may well be opening your eyes to your world as it really is. Standing at yet another of the many crossroads in your life, you are faced with a decision to make—which way do I go? I want you to see that God is at work, showing you that your uneasiness is well-founded, and there truly is something wrong. When you came to Jesus at the cross, confessed your sin, and dedicated your life to following him, you entered into real life. But through lack of dedication, ignorance, or poor teaching you have yet to understand that there is more to the Christian experience than just coming. That represents a glorious change, but it is only the beginning, just as it was for the eleven men who heard Jesus tell them to dwell in him.

Decide to Abide
What do you think about when New Year's Day comes around? Resolutions, perhaps? Most of us have made New Year's resolutions in the past, and many of us have seen them fall by the wayside soon after. Yet there was a beginning; you did make the effort to start.

In the end, most of us have to admit that the problem with sticking to resolutions was neither in resolving to do something nor beginning to do it, but the failure to do it day after day, one day at a time, every day. You didn't have a strong enough resolve to keep it up.

For example, if you needed to lose weight, it probably would take time for your metabolism to change and the pounds to start dropping off. You would notice precious little change at first, but if you set short-term goals and stuck to the plan, eventually that unwanted weight would disappear, even if you encountered times of hunger and frustration.

So it is with abiding in Jesus. Dying is the only way to receive the power of the Lord Jesus Christ to work through your life. He told his disciples that unless a grain of wheat falls into the earth and dies, it remains just one grain. It does not reproduce. But if it dies, it produces many others and yields a rich harvest.[114] This describes what the sinless Savior of humankind himself went through in order to bring you and me eternal life in him.

The natural mind reacts violently against dying to its desire to sin, which you've probably felt. But if you have sensed the Spirit trying to convince you that not everything is right in your world, you will begin to see that your current state of affairs is not what God intended. And you'll also get a glimpse of the heavenly possibilities in store.

The truly wonderful thing about walking with Jesus is seeing, with your spiritual eyes, results you never dreamed possible—if you simply purpose to walk moment by moment with him. The present moment is always the pivotal one, not the next hour's moments or tomorrow's moments. But what if you become detached from his indwelling presence for a few hours? Don't lament and say it cannot be done. Start up again right away.

For instance, when you begin to love your family with the love of Jesus, even though it may seem uncomfortable and mechanical to do so, things will start to change. Yielding to Jesus and responding in love instead of anger brings lasting results,

---

[114] John 12:24 AMP

although it may take a while for the effects to sink in. These will be worked in you as well as others, for if you stick to your resolve to abide, those mechanical actions of kindness will turn into joyful experiences while you watch God working through you as time goes by. Day by day, month by month, you will be transformed into the Master's likeness.

Never forget that your own resolve is not enough. You are weak. Acknowledge that fact to Jesus. It is up to you to believe Christ's words, die to the world, and make the choice to abide, but it is Jesus who keeps you there. He strengthens your will so you have the power to abide moment by moment. The only way to bear fruit is to abide. Hold fast to your anchor, and stand on the solid rock. Then you'll receive the rest you crave, for your anchor holds the power to keep you dead to sin and alive to do his Father's will.

Willingly choose to enter the yoke with Jesus.[115] You may wonder if this abiding life is a goal too lofty to gain, yet he says it represents the normal life of any saint in whom he dwells. It's not hard being yoked with him. On the contrary, it gives rest to your soul! Truly believing in Jesus unlocks the peace he waits to give, for in him is life and power. He said, "The words I have spoken to you—they are full of the Spirit and life."[116] The hard part is deciding to team up with him and fully buy into his offer.

When a young ox is yoked with an older, more experienced one, the pair does not operate together in harmony at first because the trainee is learning the ways of its elder. But as the learner tastes the peace and harmony of moving in accordance with the master ox, it begins to experience that comfortable feeling one feels when two work together as one.

Some may think that being yoked to Jesus and abiding in him sounds like a lot of work, but they have yet to experience the joy of Jesus in serving others. A father finds joy in teaching life lessons to his children. A mother and father experience true happiness when they see a son or daughter begin a life in Christ on his or her own, even though there were many years of effort on

---

[115] Matt. 11:29–30
[116] John 6:63

their part before that moment arrived. Helping someone to see a clearer picture of Jesus brings lasting happiness. This is what being yoked to Jesus does when he says, "Learn from me." Jesus was always giving, and the natural consequence of being yoked to him is learning to gain a giving heart.

Let's say you attend a wedding and watch the bride and groom kiss at the end of the ceremony, fulfilling a wonderful courtship in which each professed undying love for the other. They march blissfully down the aisle and out the door, faces aglow with the joy of becoming one, while greeting guests and waving to all. Then the groom gets into his car, the bride hers, and they go their separate ways to separate homes. As time goes by, they call each other daily and even get together on special occasions; otherwise they never meet unless an emergency comes up.

"Some marriage," you say. "Why don't they stay together all the time?" That's a good observation, yet we do the same thing with Jesus when, after accepting him as our Savior and professing our love for him, we worship him from afar, not as the one we are yoked to. The Bible likens our relationship with Jesus to a marriage, but how can it survive the test of time if it's only a now-and-then relationship?

Saints immersed in Jesus want even more of him, and that's a good thing. God wants you to know more of the Son, for the more you know him and his ways the more you will be like him and the more love you will give. Say good-bye to the mountain of addiction to the world's allure, and you will soon see it flung into the sea—*if* you only believe his promise, become yoked together with him, and experience the depth of his love for yourself.

Grow in grace and knowledge.[117] Abide in the Lord and begin to plumb the depths of his immense love demonstrated on Calvary. Then you will see the glory of God in the face of Jesus Christ and be changed into his likeness. Keep looking. Come to his banqueting table and dine.[118]

---

[117] 2 Peter 3:18
[118] Ps. 23:5; Song 2:4

CHAPTER 6

BEARING FRUIT

In nature, flowering plants produce fruit. When pollinated, seeds develop and are eventually scattered to take root, grow, and reproduce. There's nothing quite as attractive as ripe, colorful fruit. Just looking at a luscious, mature peach can make one's mouth water in anticipation.

What a wonderful picture of the fruit of the Spirit! Its nine beautiful segments display an attractiveness that draws people to taste of their goodness, each with its own distinctive flavor. Then, when the seeds of the indwelling Jesus are planted and take root in the good soil of a seeking, willing heart, his Spirit abides there as well.

But there is more to bringing forth fruit than meets the eye. The secret of healthy growth to maturity is found in the soil in which the vine is planted. Any plant, be it bananas or blueberries, wheat or corn, or carrots or cauliflower, depends on vital nutrients plus an adequate water supply in order to produce a quality yield. Nutritious, good-for-you fruits and vegetables are chock-full of minerals and vitamins that nurture our health and vitality.

Where do the red, ripe tomato, the green, leafy lettuce, the bright orange carrot, and the succulent strawberry get all these essential nutrients from? Out of eighteen essential nutrients, fifteen are drawn from the soil, with three extracted from the atmosphere. Each one plays a critical role in plant health, and their level in the soil greatly determines the quality of the fruit that eventually springs forth.

Becoming firmly anchored in Jesus is like being planted in rich soil. Seed scattered on hard, rocky, and thorn-covered ground doesn't give much hope for any kind of plant growth, much less any fruit. But seed sown in rich, fertile soil erupts into hardy plants that produce abundant harvests.

Do you see the parallel here? Being anchored in Jesus means you are nourished by the most productive soil possible. He will break up the hard, fallow ground of your life and remove the rocks, weeds, and thorns of pride, self, and the urge to sin. With the nutrition of the soil of the Spirit enriching your thoughts, actions, and feelings, you will then possess all the qualities anyone could ever need for living a productive life.

In stark contrast to tropical regions where plants grow tall and strong, vibrant and deep green, with luscious fruit in abundance, lies the desert. Deserts are characterized by their lack of life-giving moisture and oft-barren soil. One such wasteland, the Atacama Desert, spreads over a wide region on the western side of Peru in South America. Known as the driest area on earth, some locations there report less than one-half inch of measurable rainfall *a year*, and a few outlying weather stations have never recorded any rainfall at all!

Compared to the lush, high-rainfall regions of the world, deserts resemble a lunar landscape. The same can be said of souls devoid of life in the Holy Spirit. Such nomads roam through their days with no attachment to Christ's life-giving power and, therefore, receive and produce little or no fruit for the kingdom.

Jeremiah illustrated clearly the life of a desert dweller who trusts either in his own strength or the strength of other frail men, apart from the abiding Christ:

> Thus saith the Lord; Cursed be the man that trusteth in man, and maketh flesh his arm, and

> whose heart departeth from the Lord. For he shall be like the heath in the desert, and shall not see when good cometh; but shall inhabit the parched places in the wilderness, in a salt land and not inhabited.[119]

Supporting only small shrubs and drought-resistant plants, the desert is an arid, lonely wilderness, and so is an unfruitful life. When love, joy, peace, patience, kindness, goodness, gentleness, humility, and self-control are nonexistent, nothing of Christ blossoms in the heart. The only thing produced in such a life is the parched, dry fruit of human effort and trust in someone or something other than he who is the living water and the Bread of Life.

But add that missing moisture and nutrition that comes by believing, and what do you get?

> Blessed is the man that trusteth in the Lord, and whose hope the Lord is. For he shall be as a tree planted by the waters, and that spreadeth out her roots by the river, and shall not see when heat cometh, but her leaf shall be green; and shall not be careful in the year of drought, neither shall cease from yielding fruit.[120]

Jesus has promised to make you his dwelling place. What a promise! Why does he do this? I've said it before, but it can never be said enough; God loves everyone in the world, including you! And because he loves everyone else in the world, he lives through your words and actions so that you can bear fruit for his glory—*if* you love him and obey his command to love others. That was the mandate, objective, and joy he shared with his friends during his last night on earth—and it is yours as well.

Little or no quality fruit can ever come from branches suffering

---

[119] Jer. 17:5–6
[120] Jer. 17:7–8

from periodic soil depletion or drought. But anchored in Jesus, the Vine, we live in him and he lives in us, continually supplying our every need for leading vibrant, fruitful lives. Therefore, we can do everything as his power flows constantly through us.[121] We must always be in his presence and aware of it, just as Adam and Eve fellowshipped with God in the garden of Eden.

> The heart is deceitful above all things, and desperately wicked: who can know it? I the Lord search the heart, I try the reins, even to give every man according to his ways, and according to the fruit of his doings.[122]

Beware! We dare not trust ourselves. Only the humble will recognize that they've wandered into the desert, and only those who realize their need of help will ever find their way out. Hard-packed soil gives rise to hard hearts. Few nutrients and little water reach roots in this environment. Don't be a desert nomad. Rather than wandering your own way, run to Jesus and remain in his strong arms. Then the fruit of your labor will produce fruit that will last.

Like loosely packed, rich soil, a soft, pliable heart caresses the seeds of love and produces blossoms that burst into spiritual fruit. Founded on Jesus, and with his love flowing through your veins, your heart readily opens wide to allow that life-giving love to flow into other lives; the comfort isn't meant to stop with you. Those showers of comforting love that have fallen on you now reach out to quench the thirst of another seeking, suffering soul, like the perpetual cycle of life-giving water that evaporates, rises, condenses, and falls from the sky. Then, because they too are yoked to Jesus, that newly transformed life reaches out, and the fruit-bearing cycle continues.

What do you watch? Who do you associate with? Where do you go? How do you spend your free time? What is your purpose

---

[121] Phil. 4:13
[122] Jer. 17:9–10

in life? There really is no neutral ground. There are only two kingdoms, so it's either the Good Shepard tending you or Satan. A heart hardened because of little or no input from Jesus and constant communication with the world cannot produce long-lasting fruit, let alone thrive.[123]

Thrivers, on the other hand, have a deep assurance that everything comes from God for a purpose. When the briars of self are removed, the Spirit's purposes are fulfilled. Tragedies and trials aren't just for you or me. We are only small players among many actors, yet each role is critical, potentially altering the course of many lives and stories. We each have a choice in the decisions we make, choices that make us thrivers, survivors, or failures.

The disciples were certainly not thrivers until Pentecost. But on that momentous occasion, the Holy Spirit came into them, and their faith blossomed into everyday service for Jesus. When he comes to abide, his dynamic indwelling presence produces abundant fruit.

If you're thriving, you aren't simply surviving. Thoughts of self have been removed, and you are then set apart for God's use and become a helper instead of a hindrance. Holiness is more than an absence of moral wrong. It's the product of denying the flesh *and* becoming planted in Jesus, *then* producing fruit. Abiding in Christ activates the fruit-bearing process. The last stanza of the beloved hymn, *Have Thine Own Way*, condenses that process simply yet so beautifully:

> Have Thine own way, Lord! Have Thine own way!
>
> Hold o'er my being absolute sway!
>
> Fill with Thy Spirit till all shall see
>
> Christ only, always, living in me![124]

---

[123] 1 Cor. 15:33
[124] Adelaide Addison Pollard, "Have Thine Own Way," *https://www.hymnal.net/en/hymn/h/119* (June 1, 2015).

As you move toward fullness of faith, you will tire of having only a little of Jesus. You'll discover a yearning for your entire white-as-snow heart to be *filled* with the Spirit and emptied of the world so you can be a hundredfold fruit bearer. Then you'll be a thriver—not merely a survivor!

Singing this hymn with an honest heart denotes a person bent on turning over the right to his or her life to the living God inside. The master gardener is always nurturing the soil of your heart so it will produce fruit that will remain. Then you will be shining the light of Jesus's love wherever you go.

That lovely spiritual setting that Jeremiah extolled can be yours when you make Jesus your abode. Your life can become a veritable Eden! Belief and trust in the life-giving waters of the presence of God changes your life's landscape from desert heath to green, leafy foliage. Such an evergreen, vibrant life can be yours simply by wrapping roots of faith around your anchor.

When his Holy Spirit makes his abode in us, we are ushered into the presence of the Lord Jesus. Our Lord has a mandate from his Father to radiate the fullness of his divine, abiding life through each one of us so humankind can see, hear, and feel what God is like. To make it happen, the Spirit works constantly to show us the need to die to our self-pleasing nature so his fruit may be seen in all its glory. The fruit of the Spirit is simply the outpouring of the life of Jesus.

God has graciously planted his love in you, and if it grows, your anchor in Jesus will become stronger. Abiding in him and tended by his loving touch, you will experience the fruit of his attributes and become like him: "For me to live is Christ."[125] We will learn more about the Spirit's precious fruit in the next chapter.

---

[125] Phil. 1:21

CHAPTER 7
SPIRITUAL FRUIT

> *"But the fruit of the Spirit is love, joy, peace, forbearance, kindness, goodness, faithfulness, gentleness and self-control. Against such things there is no law."*[126]

The Fruit

Saving the world he loves motivated the inception of God's inconceivable, perplexing, yet marvelous plan to use redeemed sinners to convey his love to the lost—perplexing because God made it clear that man had no power to please him.[127] So what did he do? Jesus came to earth, died for our sin's punishment, rose victoriously over death, and ascended to heaven. *And* after he left, God sent his Holy Spirit to abide in us and give us the power to show Jesus to the world. That, my friends, is love and purpose!

The Holy Spirit is the transmitter of Christ's character. This fruit or product of the power in Jesus is heaven-sent nutrition meant to transform you into his likeness so that people will see how good he is and long to taste his lovely fruit for themselves. These nine facets of Christ that make up the fruit will mold you into his character so that the claims he makes will be proven true

---

[126] Gal. 5:22–23 NIV
[127] Col. 1:21–23

and real. God's goal is for you to be *filled* with the goodness of the Spirit.

We will take a brief look at each aspect of the Spirit's fruit, for they manifest the evidence to you and the world around you that Christ is indeed your anchor.

Love
The love between God the Father and God the Son is the very basis of the life that is in Christ Jesus. Love ranks as the first and foremost component of the precious fruit of the Spirit because the motive behind everything Jesus thinks, says, and does is born out of selfless love. This "God with us" sacrificed his life for sinful man out of a heart of love. Today, he lives in those who believe in him so they can revel in God's love and pass it on.

All the other aspects of the fruit of the Spirit flow out of love. Since God is love and the source from which love flows to you and through you to others, you are absolutely dependent upon the indwelling Spirit of Jesus for life; it can never come from anywhere else. Your Master said, "The Spirit gives life; the flesh counts for nothing."[128] Al-one, you cannot produce good fruit; therefore, you are unable to partake of God's love unless God dwells in you. It is there where fellowship with Jesus begins and grows. The only place love can be found is in coming face-to-face with the King of love.

As love's bond grows tighter and deeper, this most potent of all nutrients heals your spiritual wounds and creates a channel for Christ's fruit to flow through you into other needy lives, stimulating you to love and do good deeds for your fellow men and women by showing them Jesus. That's our purpose. Love, then, as I said, is both our personal goal and our purpose, and all the other fruits also work toward fulfilling that objective of redeeming love.

You are designed to be consumed by selfless love. Loving Christ, being loved by Christ, loving your brothers and sisters in Christ, and loving the world through Christ must be your supreme

---

[128] John 6:63

objectives. In order to fulfill his plans, this necessarily means being completely under his control.

God's nature is a selfless nature, and his glory is found in loving his creation. Since he is love and love is giving, self has no place. When Jesus came to earth, he came as a servant. Just as the Spirit of God fully inhabited Jesus when he came to seek and save that which was lost, Jesus sent his Spirit to save sinners using redeemed ones as his vessels.

Jesus came to display the love of God, and we are sent to show his love in Jesus. However, lurking in the shadows is a pretender, a counterfeit love. Paul warns us of its existence and its dangers in 1 Corinthians 13 in the parallel account of the fruit of the Spirit to our Galatians text. It can be summarized this way: *if my words and knowledge and kind deeds are not originating in the love of Christ, but in and of my own power instead, they are worthless.*

Trying to love without Christ's power guiding every step is fruitless. Henry Drummond spells it out so clearly:

> You cannot give anything more important than the Love reflected in your own life. That is the one true universal language, which allows us to speak Chinese or the dialects of India. For if, one day, you go to those places, the silent eloquence of Love will mean that you will be understood by everyone.
>
> You may accomplish everything you set out to accomplish and be prepared to make any sacrifice, but if you give your body to be burned and have not Love, you will have achieved nothing for yourself or for God's cause.[129]

It is a wonderful thing to be brought into the light of Jesus and see the beauty of his love. Suddenly, you begin to understand

---

[129] Henry Drummond, adapted by Paulo Coelho, "The Supreme Gift," *http://topshelfbook.org/wp-content/uploads/2014/02/The-Supreme-Gift-Paulo-Coelho.pdf.* (June 1, 2015).

what his grand objective has always been. But more awaits the ones who move higher on to the plane of implementation, of putting knowledge into action. To be sure, disturbances will be created by the act of giving love and living a life of self-denial as a servant, just as Jesus encountered. The Enemy is very much against displaying love. He knew what happened when the Son of God came into the world. Can you imagine his reaction to having millions of saints in the image of Jesus, loving as he loved?

Jesus, the Head of all believers everywhere, has a plan and the power to fulfill it. Each member is to function in such a way so that the entire body, receiving love and direction from the Head, moves in a purposeful, coordinated manner. Jesus is therefore not ashamed to call us brothers and sisters. He loved us enough to die for our sins so our sibling relationship with him could be established.

The body of Christ is meant to function in complete unity. The love that radiates from brothers and sisters in a human family who live and work in mutual love and dependence grabs attention, especially in this self-centered, ego-driven society in which we live. When we as believers love our spiritual kin as Jesus does, a testimony of Christ's love spreads through our neighborhoods, cities, and towns.

Joy
Joy is the complete satisfaction you feel when you are in God's presence, whether in times of fellowship or actively engaged in doing his will. Godly joy can fill your soul whenever his love is acknowledged, chosen, and exalted. Paul commended the Macedonian Christians that even though "in the midst of an ordeal of severe tribulation, their abundance of joy" led them to share what they had with others in need.[130] Jesus said we should rejoice because our names are written in heaven.

What most people mistakenly call joy is the feeling of elation that depends on outward circumstances. If someone gets an unexpected promotion, or if a student gets an A on a test, he or she

---

[130] 2 Cor. 8:2

feels elated because what he or she wanted actually came to pass. But we Christians should rejoice because our indwelling Savior walks in intimate fellowship with us—a joy the world cannot give. We have joy in our lives because God works through us to bring glory to himself. This true joy elicits Christ-directed praise, not self-directed rapture.

Rejoice that you are a recipient of the Spirit's fruit, and joy will also well up when you see the same fruit flow through you and help grow a spiritual crop in other souls for the eternal harvest. Rejoice that 1) Jesus can be trusted to bring his promises to fruition; 2) you are weak, and he is strong; 3) he is faithful to the promises he made; 4) when you are downcast, he comforts you; 5) when you are weary and heavily laden, he gives you rest; and 6) when you abide in him, he abides in you. You have so much and more in which to find joy!

Jesus is Lord, and he lives in you! Let him exercise his original intent of being everything you need in order to love him and carry out his mission. You don't need to seek for joy; it comes of its own accord when you love God and his creation. Do that, and joy in abundance will be yours.

Happiness comes and goes, but true joy is constantly active when you abide in Jesus: "The kingdom of God is not meat and drink; but righteousness, and peace, and joy in the Holy Ghost."[131]

Rejoice *in the Lord* ... always![132]

Peace

> I have told you these things, so that in Me you may have [perfect] peace and confidence. In the world you have tribulation and trials and distress and frustration; but be of good cheer [take courage; be confident, certain, undaunted]! For I have overcome the world. [I have deprived it of power to harm you and have conquered it for you.][133]

---

[131] Rom. 14:17
[132] Phil. 4:4
[133] John 16:33 AMP

So little peace. Historians can only find a few out of six thousand-plus years of recorded history with no trace of major conflict. Hatred and violence are the sad hallmarks of humanity. Jesus offers a peace the world cannot give, yet it is not merely an absence of conflict.[134] Rather, it is the state of being in a right relationship with God in an atmosphere of loving acceptance. When you are filled with the Spirit of God, you know beyond any shadow of doubt that you are loved and that you have a purpose.

Because children of the King have a goal, they possess the calm assurance that their abiding anchor gives them the tools needed to achieve it. Obediently rest in his love and obey his call to love others, and true peace will be yours. One who is at peace with his Maker is serene, open, and approachable.

When Jesus slept during the frightful storm on the sea that sent his disciples into panic, and when he was being pursued by angry Pharisees intent on killing him, he was perfectly confident that his Father loved him and had sent him with a purpose in mind. He knew whatever he faced was God's will. His relationship with his Father gave him a restful peace that saw beyond the problems of the present to a glory-filled future.

Jesus is called the Prince of Peace because he came to pay the price for humankind's sin and to bring God's healing love into the hearts of all who believe in him. The chasm separating them was closed. Peace was so paramount that when he was born, the angels sang out, "On earth peace, good will toward men."[135] The Savior, Christ the Lord, peace personified, had come.

However, when Jesus began spreading his good news, some in the multitudes who later followed him began to question the *Prince of Peace* title. He actually created conflict as he moved among men because most did not understand what true peace really was. Since the Jewish leaders could see yet were blind,[136] they only knew Jesus was disrupting their earthly definition of peace and, therefore, they sought to kill him.

---

[134] John 14:27
[135] Luke 2:14
[136] John 9:39–41

But Jesus never intended to do away with that kind of conflict. After all, he stated that he came to send a sword,[137] and even today, the peace of Jesus still can and often does cause divisions in families, churches, communities, and entire nations. People everywhere, even believers, exalt aggressive independence and power when confronting a peaceable, meek soul.

Peace on Earth and Good Will toward Men
Peace is the heart of God toward everyone. He longs to live in harmonious love with his children, yet they still create conflict. People make fun of peacemakers just as they jeered Jesus. Even many Christians cheer when problems are met with might instead of peace. If our Lord experienced hatred and rejection for enduring the same thing, we can expect it too.

"Blessed are the peacemakers,"[138] said Jesus. When he abides in you, peace like a river—the river of living water, the Holy Spirit—flows outward from you to a restless, chaotic world. Over time, people will sense a different power working in you from what the world displays. They will recognize peace as not just a transient quality in your life, but one flowing continuously in good times and bad, in calm or conflict. Remember, Jesus overcame the world, and this knowledge motivated the writer of Hebrews to exclaim, "I will not fear what man shall do unto me."[139]

Men and women immersed in the pursuit of pleasure, success, and other self-centered goals have no peace with the Lord; therefore, they are subject to conflict instead. "The natural, nonspiritual man does not accept or welcome or admit into his heart the gifts and teachings and revelations of the Spirit of God, for they are folly (meaningless nonsense) to him."[140]

On the other hand, humble people have no reputation of their own to uphold, only that of their Lord. They never get into arguments over whom or what is better or worse. They simply

---

[137] Matt. 10:34
[138] Matt. 5:9
[139] Heb. 13:6
[140] 1 Cor. 2:14 AMP

set their minds on loving and helping. Such people shine like a beacon through a dark and dreary night, for they possess the peace that passes understanding. So take courage; be confident, certain, and undaunted—for Jesus has overcome the world and anything it can do![141]

Patience
If you can endure lengthy periods of suffering of any kind, you are a patient person. In fact, patience is translated *long-suffering* in the *King James Bible*. Suffering comes in many forms, from waiting in a long checkout line to dealing with a chronic disease to enduring verbal abuse, and is the key to successfully riding through whatever storms you encounter. You give clear evidence of the power of Jesus working in you if you can display the fruit of the Spirit in the face of extended difficulties.

Jesus is patience personified. As an example, he displayed infinite forbearance with Peter during their three-year journey together. Peter once denied he even knew Jesus after boasting he would never leave his Lord, yet Jesus reacted with patience: "You will deny me, but when you return, love your brothers."[142]

When no power to overcome on your own is strong enough to meet the deep need, handling stressful times such as laboriously caring for a mentally or physically impaired loved one, waiting for word from a dear friend who cannot be found, or lying on a sickbed testify to the inner presence of Christ. If you rely on Jesus, these and any other situations of strain and stress will deepen your faith and produce an amazed wonder in observers. Patience beautifully displays the love of Jesus to everyone, as you yourself have experienced. Think of those special encounters with people who have patiently listened to your problems as you poured out your own heart to them.

Forgiveness and patience are closely related. Just think how patiently your Lord has worked to transform you into his loving image despite times of your disobedient behavior. A patient person

---
[141] Phil. 4:7
[142] John 13:36–38

constantly remembers that God loves, forgives, and refines despite any shortcomings. That's the kind of patience we're talking about. Remembering Christ's love and patience will make you all the more eager to let his power patiently work through you to show the same long-suffering forbearing love to others. Then, if you've been wronged, you won't snap back in reply, but respond with understanding instead.

God never grows weary of molding you into his image. It's often your own lack of a patient heart during the process that hinders your progress and, hence, your usefulness. Cooperate with him, for he has chosen to glorify himself by creating you with the ability to choose love for others instead of your own desires.

Impatient people butt into conversations with their views. They make decisions without considering the outcome and seldom, if ever, consult Jesus about issues. They want results *now*. They want prayer answered *now*. Impatience is a fruit of the flesh and works against love because the "I, me, mine" syndrome always supersedes other people's needs. Such people are rigid, inflexible in their selfish attitudes and actions.

Jesus was always patiently flexible. Many times he welcomed the ones his disciples tried to shoo away. He often deviated from his destination to heal, encourage, and do loving deeds. Consider the Lord's parable of the good Samaritan. Now there's flexibility. Everything connected with that good-deed doer revealed a heart intent on meeting needs other than his own. Jesus will not tolerate those who do not show patient love. He says, *Do this [love the Lord and your neighbor] and you will live.*[143]

Flexible people have soft, pliable hearts searching for a need and do all they can to meet it. We all display the virtues of patient love at times. But the deeper we abide and the stronger we grip the rope of faith connecting us to our anchor, the more the Spirit's patience will bless needy souls.

The patience of God goes far beyond the mere putting up with we often practice. Think of a mother's love as she deals with her children. This is especially true of those wonderful mothers who

---

[143] Read Luke 10:25–37.

have a special-needs child. They've poured so much of themselves into this child's life, you might say part of them lives inside the child. The same can be said of you too as you patiently give the love of Jesus without reservation.

How do you gain patience? First, turn your eyes away from the allurement of the world and look at Jesus, the source of your faith and the one who brings patience to maturity and perfection. He patiently suffered for you and daily bears with you to bring his purposes to fruition. Ask him to bless you with his long-suffering character.

Then strip off every encumbrance and sin, for all the excess baggage that ties you to this earth—worries, distrust, and the like—prevent you from living in Christ's power. Our Savior saw his goal ahead, rejoiced in the ultimate joy of seeing many brothers and sisters dwelling in heaven with him for eternity, and patiently endured horrible hardships to reach it.

Finally, look at others through Jesus's eyes and let his love flow. Keep focusing on his presence, and his marvelous might will keep you from growing tired and losing heart so that you may rejoice with him. Then, my friend, you will have patience.

Kindness
Caring is at the core of kindness. Philip Keller pictured kindness this way: "We are moved to be kind because we care. Caring is the essence of God's selfless love expressed to another."[144]

Kindness radiates the warmth of the human soul to someone in need. Whether the need be great or small, a kind deed triggered by a heart filled with Christ's love generates more potential for good than a chest filled with gold. Think of times when someone explained the meaning of a passage from the Bible or gave you a deeper insight into the love of Jesus. Perhaps a stranger helped you when your car broke down.

Almost anyone, saved or not, can do a good deed, even one for which they get little or no recognition. But God's kindness

---

[144] Philip Keller, *A Gardener Looks at the Fruits of the Spirit* (Waco, TX: Word Books, 1979).

always has both our eternal good and the good of others in view. Kindness, as a facet of God's love, gives and comforts within the framework of Christ's goal—fitting the needy with purpose and for heaven. It's a merciful act, driven by God's love. True Holy Spirit kindness gives to everyone, with the goal in mind of showing them Jesus, regardless of who it is or what his or her background may be.

A kind person is tender, compassionate, sweet, and observant. Opportunities abound to show a caring heart in this world of hatred, sadness, violence, divorce, immorality, homelessness, sickness, and poverty. Just look around.

Jesus makes loving compassion a clear must if we say we love him:

> Then shall the King say unto them on his right hand, Come, ye blessed of my Father, inherit the kingdom prepared for you from the foundation of the world: For I was an hungered, and ye gave me meat: I was thirsty, and ye gave me drink: I was a stranger, and ye took me in: Naked, and ye clothed me: I was sick, and ye visited me: I was in prison, and ye came unto me … Inasmuch as ye have done it unto one of the least of these my brethren, ye have done it unto me.[145]

However, Jesus promised dire consequences if we turn away from deep needs, for compassionate, comforting love is the character of the King, and the servant must be as his master. For instance, the busyness of our lives cripples our efforts to be kind because it robs us of one of our greatest allies—time. We often succumb to what some have called "the tyranny of the urgent." Allowing the "needs" and "have-to's" of our lives to have a higher priority than showing love whenever the opportunity arises is unacceptable in the sight of God.

You have a meeting you have to attend, but a friend just called pleading for help because his wife is desperately ill, or maybe

---

[145] Matt. 25:34–40

you come upon someone stranded in a car as you speed to your doctor's appointment. Jesus will be faithful to give you countless similar opportunities to show you care—*if* you care. God will always show us how to correctly order our lives *if* we abide in him.

Jesus paid the ultimate price—the best laying down his life for the worst—and he expects us to lay down our lives for others:

> For you know the grace of our Lord Jesus Christ, that though he was rich, yet for your sakes he became poor, that you through his poverty might be rich.[146]

> Be kind and compassionate to one another, forgiving each other, just as in Christ God forgave you. Be imitators of God, therefore, as dearly loved children and live a life of love, just as Christ loved us and gave himself up for us as a fragrant offering and sacrifice to God.[147]

The sin of unkindness draws God's wrath. But kindness, compassion, and love come from God's heart and are offerings fragrant with the dew of a sweet-smelling sacrifice.

Goodness
Goodness is the essence of holiness as opposed to evil: it's related to purity of thought and action. Everything God does is good, even though it may not always reflect kindness toward an individual. When Jesus healed a blind man, he was showing both goodness and kindness. However, when he berated the Jewish leaders for being angry that a man was healed on the Sabbath, he was still showing goodness.

Jesus said there was only one who was good, so all goodness, as with the other facets of the Spirit's fruit, flows from him. Peter testified that Jesus went about doing good.[148] Whether it was

---

[146] 2 Cor. 8:9
[147] Eph. 4:32; 5:1–2
[148] Acts 10:38

teaching, interacting, praying, or performing miraculous signs, whatever he said or did was good.

You, I, and every believer in Christ can testify to the Lord's goodness. Saving us from spending eternity separated from Jesus; leading us through trials to fit us for his kingdom: whatever he does, he does all things well.

Remember, good deeds only come through God's power, and they aren't optional. You don't *earn* your salvation by doing them, but they please the Lord and bear precious fruit, especially when you bless fellow saints. It is easy to shy away from showing this quality of the Spirit's fruit because doing good takes time and energy. But the more good you do for others, the more you are encouraged and strengthened as the Spirit of Christ gives you a greater supply of real life.

We are admonished to "do good [morally] to all people [not only being useful or profitable to them, *but also doing what is for their spiritual good and advantage]*. Be mindful to be a blessing, especially to those of the household of faith."[149]

You may have been treated wrongly by a friend, maybe even one who is a fellow believer. Only the great love of Jesus can keep you doing good to those who mistreat you. Praying for the spiritual good of that person transforms your attitude and may impact his or her life for good. The Lord may tell you to speak the truth to that person for his or her benefit, but do it in Christ's love.

You will be known by your fruit, says the Lord. If you sow to your own interests, you will reap "decay and ruin and destruction." If, on the other hand, you scatter the seeds of the Spirit, you'll reap eternal life with Jesus.[150] You were reborn in Christ Jesus for this very purpose. For that reason, don't grow weary of doing good deeds and give up. Someday, maybe sooner than you think, you will receive that eternal reward of being with your Lord face-to-face if you don't give up.[151]

---

[149] Gal. 6:10 AMP
[150] Gal. 6:7–8 AMP
[151] Gal. 6:9

Faithfulness
I've already stressed the importance of believing in Jesus Christ and his authoritative words. But faith as a fruit of the Spirit points all around us on this earth as well. God is always faithful to you, therefore, be faithful to others. In Christ there is no shadow or variableness in turning, so remain true to your word and promises. Jesus has faith that you can be conformed to his image, so believe others can do the same.

Jesus gives you faith in the first place; you must simply believe and act on it. Look upon your fellow man with the eyes of Christ and begin to see potential for good. Then invest the other components of God's gift to lead them to Christ or to strengthen the seed that may already be there.

The Lord Jesus demonstrated faith in his disciples over and over again, even though they often let him down. Paul commended the Ephesians and the Thessalonians repeatedly for their demonstration of faith and the love that poured out of it. He also told the Romans that he prayed they would be "mutually strengthened and encouraged and comforted" by each other's faith.[152]

Since marriage is a symbol of our relationship with Christ, faithfulness between husband and wife is essential. Truth to one's word gives powerful evidence of the abiding Christ in your life. Having faith in your spouse reassures your mate of your love. In addition, a faithful, loving parent recognizes the inevitability of ungodly behavior occurring in their children that must be dealt with at some point. But still they seek to encourage, exhort, and rebuke them and lead them into a life that glorifies the Lord Jesus.

You, no doubt, appreciate working under a person who encourages you. He or she may point out your errors, but he or she does it because he or she wants to make you better at what you are doing, not to put you in your place. Such people have your best interests at heart. God wants your faith to increase, but the increase must come from God. He wants you to trust him more,

---

[152] Rom. 1:12

and others as well, so that much more fruit can be reaped in their lives as their faith increases.

Gentleness

When someone gently cares for a sick child or carefully helps an elderly person, that person displays humility and meekness. Putting aside his or her own plans, that person stoops to help the lowly and meet the needs of those who cannot help themselves. Unlike self-centered people, who often push their own agenda and come across as loud and egotistical, a gentle person promotes God's understanding, unselfish servant heart and projects compassion.

People endued with the gentleness of Jesus are empathetic. That means they identify with another person's struggles. They walk a mile in the hurting or defenseless person's shoes. Gentle people see the world through others' eyes and feel their pain and suffering.

This quality was personified in our Lord, Jesus Christ, the King of all creation and yet so meek. He was the humble Lamb of God and the Good Shepherd, a gentle-hearted man who encouraged children to sit on his knee. Everything about him spoke of self-*less*-ness. His birth, family, friends, and surroundings all identified Jesus as one who lived to serve God and man, and not himself.[153]

Look around you today, and what do you see? A society crippled by an emphasis on self-esteem and self-fulfillment. *Be self-assured and self-sufficient!* Sadly, the evidence of living for self runs rampant in the church as well. But, *deny yourself and be a servant,* says Jesus. *Learn from me,* says the Lord of the universe. However, his pleas are difficult to heed when all around voices cry out, *Please yourself! You deserve a break! Celebrate you!*

Meek men and women are not weak. When they are strong in the Lord and operate by the power of his Spirit, they simply radiate a mild manner infused with gentleness. Those who think that strength is measured by asserting one's will and demanding

---

[153] Mark 10:45

one's rights call such gentleness a weakness, which is a false assumption. True strength is found in saying no to your own power and yes to the Lord's desire to work his mighty power through you.[154] Remember, the meek are the ones who shall inherit the earth.[155]

Self-control
Self-control is simply this: putting your *self* under the control of Jesus. You are not simply obeying a set of rules; you are listening to and heeding the impulse of Jesus telling you what his will is in every situation life can offer.

A person under Christ's control moves into the yoke with him and chooses to be a channel of action for the Holy Spirit's fruit. Rather than having a flair for the exciting and daring activities this world offers, this person puts his or her heart and soul into the adventure of following in the footsteps of his or her Master.

When Christ walked on earth, he spoke and acted under the control of his Father at all times. Healing a pathetic, demon-possessed man by the sea; speaking to a seeking woman by a well; teaching his new disciples on a sun-drenched hillside; angrily chastising Jewish leaders at the temple: in each and every instance he followed God's perfect will.

What would be your reaction if you were faced with a situation as Jesus was when a Pharisee invited him for dinner? During the meal, when a woman interrupted them and anointed the Lord's feet, the Pharisee reacted with indignation because Jesus didn't condemn her sinful past. Most Christians reading this account would react in what some would call righteous anger and berate the Pharisee for his "unholy" attitude. But Jesus had put himself under his Father's control, and so he saw a beautiful teaching opportunity. As a result, the man ended up convicting himself of his lack of true love.[156]

---

[154] 2 Cor. 12:9–10
[155] Matt. 5:5
[156] Luke 7:36–50

Conclusion

Jesus possessed all of these spiritual qualities of the heavenly perfection of his Holy Spirit when he was on earth and lived them out to their fullest extent and purpose. We can believe his promise to use us as vessels to pass on his life of loving kindness to others. Abiding in Christ and living a fruitful life is the hallmark of normal Christian life.

Our Lord wants to raise up passionate people who long to be like him by partaking of the fruit he offers. He himself exhibited passion as he brought God's love to the world through his deeds, teaching, and his testimony. He was passionate about people and their eternal destiny. He was passionate about communing with his Father. He experienced and gave love continually, and he wanted people everywhere to know that God is love.

Abiding in Jesus places the anchor of our souls within our hearts and opens the gate for the fruit of his Spirit to fill every bit of our lives and pour out into the lives of all we meet. In this way, with the fruit of his life coursing through you, more hungry, searching, desperate souls can be anchored in his love.

PART 3

ANCHORED TO LOVE

CHAPTER 8

ANCHORED FOR A PURPOSE

"Purpose: the aim or goal of a person: what a person is trying to do, become."[157]

The multitudes marveled when they saw Jesus bringing healing love to common, everyday people, and they glorified God for it. Jesus wants to love through you, for millions today need his life-giving touch. We are no longer dealing with an historical Jesus and what he said in the past. He is a living, abiding Lord whose words are eternal, so I long for you to understand how this living power can work out your purpose for the glory of our Savior and God.

"And we know that all things work together for good to them that love God, to them who are the called according to his purpose."[158]

We've come a long way in learning why Jesus must be our anchor, and if you have believed him, this eternal Christ now

---

[157] *Merriam-Webster* Online Dictionary, http://www.merriam-webster.com/dictionary/purpose (June 1, 2015).
[158] Rom. 8:28

abides in you. But before we launch into the most critical part of my burden, let's review the previous chapters, since those facts are crucial to understanding God's purpose. This is where we move from history to practice:

- Jesus came as God in man to bring his Father's love into the hearts of sinners who confess their evil ways and believe in him. He humbled himself and took on the likeness of a man to bring life, real life, to humankind—God's life. That genuine life, what man was created to be, is found in Jesus alone, and he gives that life to whoever believes and follows him.
- Believing was a constant theme of our Lord, for he had the words of God to share with whoever would hear his voice. Believing Christ's message was the key to unlocking all the treasures of the life God wanted to give.
- Jesus came to abide in those who believed through his Holy Spirit. His continual presence brings overcoming power into dead lives to defeat sin and Satan.
- Jesus came to empower his servants to bear fruit. Through them, he continues to give life to the lost.

Throw out any definition of love other than this one: God is love. Our anchor and Creator is a God of love. Everything he brought into existence perfectly reflected the love of the Father and his Son, Jesus Christ, until sin entered and marred it all. Jesus came into our corrupted human environment and lived God's love to teach us what God required so we might receive the eternal bliss in which man was intended to live. Eventually, he was crucified as payment for our sin. But he rose victorious over death, sin, and the grave and sent his Holy Spirit so that he himself could live in those who believed in him and give them power to live for God. That, in a nutshell, was his purpose for coming.

God saved you and called you, not because of any good works you have done, but because he has always had a purpose for the church—all believers—that he planned before the world began: to give the good news that Jesus has brought light and everlasting life to whoever will receive him.[159] No matter who you are, spreading the message that Jesus Christ is Lord, is love, is the way, the truth, and the life, and that all things point to him, sums up your calling no matter who you are. He is the heart of God.

I trust that at this point you understand that Jesus led a purpose-driven life and that he now dwells in us. Now, if these two statements are true, it follows that he will have the same goals for you as the Father had for him. You must understand what your *purpose* in life is so that you fully experience and utilize the fruit of the Spirit. You have to understand your calling before you can live it.

Believe it
Earlier, we focused at length on the importance Jesus placed on continually believing in him, and for good reason: it unlocks the treasure of all he can and will do. Believing in the abiding presence of Jesus must take place before his power to accomplish your purpose can be released. If you don't consistently believe, the acceptance and purpose you are searching for will always elude you.

Ignoring Jesus's commands or just paying them lip service brings the death sentence to the fruit of his Spirit. Without bearing fruit, we can do nothing to please him. And we can't expect to have more of Christ's character and be truly useful servants in his kingdom while working at it only part-time, if at all. Believing is a full-time job. As an example, consider the following scenario.

Joe had experienced trouble catching his breath for several years. His doctor ordered tests, which confirmed both his feelings and Joe's worst fears; several arteries in his heart were filled with plaque. Joe needed coronary bypass surgery immediately or faced a certain heart attack.

The complex operation went according to plan. Joe recovered quickly, and the doctor then placed him on blood pressure and cholesterol-lowering drugs to prevent the same problem from

---
[159] 2 Tim. 1:9–10

cropping up again. But he cautioned Joe to take the medication daily in order for it to be effective. If he didn't heed the instructions, another operation might have to be performed.

If you were Joe, wouldn't you take your medication regularly as prescribed? Of course you would, or you'd be facing another open-heart ordeal. You would carefully follow the medication directions, making sure you never missed a dose and take it at the time of day it was prescribed. If you did forget, you'd make sure not to do it again because you would always be painfully aware of the consequences.

However, were you to repeatedly miss doses, you would soon discover that your body had no toleration for absentmindedness. When you had your next checkup, you'd discover your blood pressure would have risen dramatically.

It's no different with believing. If you are a follower of Christ, at some time in the past the great physician diagnosed your lack of spiritual vitality—your fear, doubt, fascination with this world, and dependence on self-effort—as eventually fatal coronary disease. You trusted in his mercy and love, and so he performed surgery and gave you a new heart. When you awoke he wrote out a prescription for the only medication that would keep your heart disease from returning—*continual belief and reliance on the indwelling presence of Jesus Christ.*

In order to be truly effective, God's prescribed medication also must be taken continuously. It makes sense, doesn't it? Countless hymns and songs we sing are built around the need to make Jesus everything. You simply cannot do anything without him; it takes full commitment: "Love so amazing, so divine, demands my soul, my life, my all."[160]

But those sentiments, accurate as they are, need your action in order to realize the fellowship you long for. Believing opens

---

[160] Isaac Watts, "When I Survey the Wondrous Cross," *http://www.hymnsite.com/lyrics/umh298.sht* (June 1, 2015).

bruised, hurting hearts to the balm in Gilead for the great physician to heal.[161] It is the only remedy that will satisfy your longing for fellowship with Jesus. Then you will be whole-hearted, a useful servant in your dear Lord's kingdom, one who shows the completeness of God's love to other saints and a lost world searching for life.

When Jesus told the crowd that unless they ate his flesh and drank his blood they would have no part in him, his listening disciples grew uneasy, and some turned away. Jesus looked at the twelve and asked them point-blank if they would leave as well. But instead of departing, they replied out of their confusion, "Lord, to whom shall we go? You have the words of eternal life."[162] They didn't understand the deeper meaning of those words at that time, but they did express faith in Jesus. True, it was a very small, weak faith—a mustard seed faith—but it was enough to keep them going until the power of the Spirit of Jesus came upon them.

You too may be restless and not understand what Jesus is trying to do in and through you. But the question still is, do you believe? Believe and rest in Jesus's promises and assurance no matter what you are facing, be it simple or complicated, painless or agonizing. Always respond in obedience to his impulse, regardless of where you think it may lead.

A mountain of unbelief may be blocking your entrance into the deeper Christian life. Simply humble yourself and say, *Christ lives in me*, and it will begin to disappear. Soon, instead of being hindered by unbelief, you will be standing atop a mountain of faith.

Operating on a spiritual plane and unleashing all that Jesus is and will do in your life is simple—believe him. That is the key. This standard for entrance into a life filled with peace and purpose is repeated over and over by Jesus himself in the Gospels, and later by the post-Resurrection writers. It's all about faith.

Simply put, being spiritual means someone else has taken

---

[161] Jer. 8:22
[162] John 6:66–69 NKJV

up residence and is directing your thoughts and actions. How spiritual you are depends on how much of your life the Spirit of Christ controls. Always remember this fundamental fact that Jesus is setting before you: without him, you can do nothing. Never forget that, and never stop believing that he is there doing what he promised.

Strengthen the Believing Rope
Until modern times, rope lines called hawsers, sometimes as big around as a strong man's arm, were often used on large ships for dropping the anchor at sea. A hawser was actually several small ropes braided tightly together to form one thick, massive line, and it served its purpose even under strong winds and currents.

Although a fledgling faith will accomplish great things through Jesus, he asks for entire constant consecration and availability, requiring a continually strong belief in his mighty indwelling power. Adding more acts of faith to your experience is like adding more strands of rope to the line until it becomes a hawser; the stronger your faith, the stronger the link between you and your resident anchor and the more he will accomplish through you. Seeing Jesus answer prayer, heal, or bring change increases faith's strands.

A living thing is designed to grow and reproduce. Out of a weak faith, a belief in the power of Christ can grow that becomes a mountain itself. Consider Paul, the apostle. All the trials and tribulation he endured to successfully spread the gospel came from his belief that when he admitted he was weak, he was actually strong through Jesus.[163] His unswerving faith and devotion opened him up to be used in a mighty way by his indwelling Lord.

To gain a hawser-strong faith, say to Jesus, *I believe you died to pay the penalty for my sins and rose from the grave, breaking the bonds of death. I believe you ascended to heaven and now sit at the right hand of your Father. I believe you sent your Spirit to give me power to live above sin so that I can do your work. I believe your grace is sufficient for me. I believe you are living in me. I believe that without you, I am helpless.*

---

[163] 2 Cor. 12:10

Then believe he heard you and believe he will act in you—and do it often!

Jesus brings his life and purpose to humankind, and it must well up in you. Since he stated he is the center of all things—and his is the voice of authority telling you how to live—this you must believe and honor. He does not demand anything; instead, he offers a life of genuine love, purpose, and a future—his life, his future, and his purpose in us.

Being anchored in Christ begins and ends with believing—a true, active faith. Look at how the *Amplified Bible* expands the meaning of the word *believe* in John 20:31 (emphasis mine):

But these are written (recorded) in order that you may *believe* that Jesus is the Christ (the Anointed One), the Son of God, and that through *believing* and cleaving to and trusting and relying upon Him you may have life through (in) His name [through Who He is].

Please notice the powerful terms that help us see the full picture of what believing means:

- *cleaving to*—holding on to Jesus for dear life, if you will.
- *trusting*—never doubting, always confident of his actions in you.
- r*elying*—counting on what Jesus has said and done in every moment and experience you live through.

Elsewhere the *Amplified Bible* uses the word *adhere* to describe believing. This term pictures the tightest possible bond between two objects—super-glued. When you believe, you are bonded to Jesus much as a bond-servant was, of his own choice, bound to his master.

Finally, the source of your faith:

- *through (in) his name [through who he is]*—his name takes in everything Jesus is, stands for, and says.

Love to Christ and the World

You play a crucial role in God's plan to redeem the world, and what a privilege it is to be a standard bearer for the King! Your love for Jesus, however, is dependent on obedience to all his commandments, for holiness frees you from the bondage of sin and allows Jesus free reign to love through you. It's fine to say you love him and to sing his praises. But it's when you, with a contrite heart, willingly give him full rein to love others through you that your Lord is truly glorified. Love, joy, peace, and patience flowing from a vessel set apart for his use can then be poured into other willing hearts around the world.

What a privilege to help someone to heaven! It's truly a tremendous task and will be accomplished through many, but *you* will be used for his glory only if the loving Jesus does the work through *your* mouth, eyes, hands, and feet. And that is why believing is so very crucial.

Maybe allowing Jesus to control your life to meet that goal appears difficult. But never forget he said, "My yoke is easy, and my burden is light."[164] If you believe and act on your faith, he will lift you up and strengthen you, and your life will change one good deed at a time. The more you love, the easier it becomes to love again and again. The spirit of liberty will set you free; you are free indeed when you set your affection on Jesus and yield to his power.

Jesus stated that those who loved him would keep his commandments, and many of them are centered on loving others. It's not our verbal profession alone but our Spirit-powered deeds that testify to his greatness. Lots of people *talk* about the fruit of the Spirit; but it's the *walk* that counts. It starts with loving other Christians. Together we are the Lord's army, and our captain directs much of the Spirit's life-giving fruit into our lives through other saints. When another brother or sister in Christ shows kindness to us mixed with gentleness and patience, that power of Jesus abiding and working through their lives strengthens and encourages us to love them in the same way for Christ's glory.

When you believe and abide, the door swings open to being

---

[164] Matt. 11:30

used by the Lord Jesus to love the world. You are walking in the Spirit. But as I've suggested, walking in the Spirit is a moment-by-moment experience requiring moment-by-moment decisions, for the Evil One continually bombards you with temptations to follow him and his ways. Having a quiet time in the morning is not enough to keep him at bay. Satan does not relax his efforts just because you have started the day right.

When you made the choice to follow Jesus, his perfect nature came to dwell in you; however, your old sinful self has not lost its power. Even though born again, you still possess the choice to serve God or to serve Satan. Thankfully, the resident Spirit of Jesus Christ patiently awaits continual contact with you twenty-four hours a day. When you hear the Holy Spirit's voice, another direction may tempt you—the way of sin. At that moment you can humbly say with total confidence, *Jesus, you are my shepherd. I will follow you!* Make that a precept for life.

You will be giving up something to be consumed by Christ, but look at what you'll get in return: Jesus as your anchor. You don't need your own judgment; you do need obedience coupled with faith in Jesus in order to gain all he promises, because only he can explain, teach, and perform. It has to be God and him alone as the ruling force in your life, not *I'll do this*, or *I'll do that*. You constantly need the Savior and his power.

Have doubts and fears ever derailed your choice to obey Jesus? The solution is to simply affirm your conviction, however weak it may be: *I believe you, Lord, and I choose to follow you.* When you are anchored by faith in the Lord's ways, the power to do what Jesus tells you wells up within so that you can carry out his leading. In effect, you say no to sin, yes to service, and put your Master's bidding into action.

Your entire relationship with God is built upon Jesus Christ; he will do all he can to teach you to trust him. He searches your heart and brings whatever contradicts your thoughts, words, and actions into the light so that you can deal with it and make the connection more secure. We don't realize how much we trust in ourselves, but the Holy Spirit's pure light makes everything clear.

Jesus continually reminds you of his presence and his willingness to guide you. Each obedient act increases your awareness so that, alongside the ever-present temptations to go your own way, you are more aware of the still, small voice calling you to go his way. This process is actually rather simple, but after years of following a different drummer, our sinful natures want to listen to the old beat and not the new. Ignorance breeds fear and doubt, so we hesitate to turn everything over to Jesus and rely on his strength. Perhaps you've never truly attempted to abandon your own ways, which is the necessary prerequisite to experiencing his love and power. Just let go, even in a small way, and watch what happens.

In time, after you've been blessed beyond measure by seeing and experiencing the effects of abiding in Christ, you will continually walk the paths he wants you to tread. Blessed peace will be yours, and real joy will flood your soul when you love and feel loved and accepted by your beloved Savior.

Love and the Ephesians
Shortly before our Lord was arrested that fateful night, he prayed to his Father for those for whom he was going to die:

> I have given to them the glory and honor which You have given Me, that they may be one [even] as We are one: I in them and You in Me, in order that they may become one and perfectly united, that the world may know and [definitely] recognize that You sent Me and that You have loved them [even] as You have loved Me.[165]

Paul's letter to the church at Ephesus demonstrated that love for each other and the world is God's will for his children. Let's look at Paul's heart as he poured it out to these saints, and we'll see our Lord's purpose clearly, for his message reflects the heart of God for you as well.[166]

---

[165] John 17:22–23 AMP
[166] Please read the entire epistle of Paul to the Ephesians.

Paul knew Jesus loved the Ephesian believers, and because of God's wonderful plan, their love for each other would be the evidence that the mighty power of Jesus was behind it. In addition, the Spirit's gentleness, goodness, and the rest of his fruit would inspire onlookers to seek such love for themselves.

Paul gave thanks that the Ephesians were, in fact, demonstrating their faith and love[167] and prayed that God would draw them ever deeper into experiencing the power of Christ. When Jesus dwell's in the heart of one walking with him in deepest humility and meekness, his deep and mighty love displays all the fruits of the Spirit. The needs of brothers and sisters in Christ are met because we truly love them. That love unites all of us and fits us for his purpose.[168]

The saints, says Paul, should strive for the height of Christ's own perfection (as it says in the *Amplified Bible*), which is the measure of his fullness in us.[169] And in perfecting one another—speaking the truth in love and edifying and encouraging one another—the body of Christ strengthens itself toward full maturity, when everyone comes to a blessed complete unity.

Because of the beauty of the Lord's plan, Christians must flee all forms of evil and not participate with those who are involved in evil pursuits because, even though we did those things in the past, we are now the light of the Lord for others.[170] We must walk in the fruit of the Spirit because this alone is acceptable with God.

Our hearts should especially go out to the weak in faith, taking every opportunity to give a boost to their vision of Jesus abiding in them. Helping brothers or sisters in Christ who are weak and subject to sin fulfills the law of Christ to love one another.[171]

Whatever we invest our time in, we will reap something. If we spend our lives on the things of this world, we will end in failure, but if we walk in the power of Jesus Christ, our reward will be eternal life. Because of that sobering thought, we should never

---

[167] Eph. 1:15–16
[168] Eph. 4:10
[169] Eph. 4:12–16
[170] 5:3–14
[171] Gal. 6:2–9

tire or give up letting Christ love through us. So we must keep doing good to everyone, and especially those who are part of God's family.[172] We have nothing to boast about except that Jesus died on the cross for us. For his sake and through his power, the world has been crucified to us and we to the world.[173]

Paul knew of the unseen presence of the Prince of Darkness and exhorted the Ephesians to be on their guard. Life is a battleground, and we are fighting a fierce foe bent on destroying anyone and anything that stands for his arch-enemy—Jesus Christ. Therefore, we need to put on armor—a metaphor for Jesus that Paul also used to encourage the Roman believers.[174]

The apostle to the Gentiles finished his letter by encouraging the saints to continually meet together to encourage and exhort one another. But remember, taking an interest in someone's life requires time and effort. One-half hour of casual visiting after Sunday's service isn't what Jesus has in mind. We need continual fellowship with his abiding power in order to display the fruit of the Spirit that keeps us strong in the faith.

Tragically, whatever the church at Ephesus learned from Paul's epistle was eventually lost. Read John's Revelation of Jesus Christ, and you will find Jesus was then about to remove his presence from them because they had left their first love. Though they still did good deeds, their acts of kindness were being carried out by their own power; Jesus was on the outside looking in. But still he longed to regain the position from which he had been driven, and so he mercifully offered to renew the fellowship that had been lost. With Jesus abiding and reigning in their hearts, they would overcome the world.[175]

How Fruit Changes the Lost
God loved you so much that he gave his dearest and best to buy you back; you were that precious to him. That sums up the heart

---

[172] Gal. 6:10
[173] Gal. 6:14
[174] Eph. 6:11–18; Rom. 13:14
[175] Rev. 2:1–7

of God and your purpose in one brief yet powerful statement. Jesus came not to do his own will but his Father's. Since that heart attitude motivated the God of eternity, and you are created in his image, giving up yourself in order to live for others becomes *your* purpose as well.

Every step of the way and at every turn, the heart of Jesus was locked into giving the fullness of his love to undeserving sinners. His compassion ran so deep that he wept when he looked back at Jerusalem and considered where the choice of its inhabitants to reject him would lead. That's how much he loved them; it's how much he loves you and every soul that was ever born.

God never intended, however, that you should only be on the receiving end of his love. Love is not love until it is given, so to be only loved and not giving love thwarts his purpose. You are a message-bearer to spread this good news. And just like your Lord, you carry that message to men and women by what you say and do and the compassion you evidence.

Paul exhorted the Corinthians to *comfort* one another, employing the same word Jesus used to refer to the Holy Spirit—the *Comforter*. Paul told them God was showing his love by comforting them through hard times. But he went on to say they then had a responsibility to comfort others themselves. Therefore, the fruit of the Spirit of Christ in us not only meets our every need but also flows out to those we influence.[176]

God has certainly comforted you in numerous ways in the past, hasn't he? And he likely used other Christians as vessels of his comfort to meet your need, perhaps through an apt word, a kind deed, a gift, or thoughtful gesture of some sort; perhaps prayer on your behalf. God produces that fruit *in* you so he can send it *through* you. His love is felt by the kindness in your voice and the gentleness of your touch. Patient forbearance and acceptance are seldom to be found, so when you help someone who has wronged you, they too experience the love of Jesus. Then, when people ask why you are so kind and caring, you point them to the source.

---

[176] 2 Cor. 1:3–7

Your Mission

Before he ascended to heaven, Jesus commissioned his first disciples to spread out and begin to reach the world with the good news of his love. Over the centuries, that swelling tide has reached into every corner of the world and brought people from widely divergent backgrounds, including you, into the family of God.

As a result of this global movement, you have a responsibility to love all Christians—not just those in your own community or country. Many of them live in lands where millions of souls have never even heard the name of Jesus. They labor under the yoke of repressive religious systems and suffer extreme poverty and, often, persecution. Especially on the Lord's heart are those who are persecuted and imprisoned for following him.[177]

Focus on strengthening Christ's worldwide body for the task of shining as lights in their own lands. The Holy Spirit is leading a tremendous turnaround, and many are committing their lives to Jesus and experiencing his light and peace for the first time. Some people have money to give to further the kingdom, but everyone can pray with sincerity, understanding, and compassion. Prayer is a vital component of your purpose.

Jesus had a mission for Paul when he grabbed his attention on the road to Damascus, and he has one for you as well, both at home and abroad. Think of what Paul did in strengthening the saints after he won them for Christ: all the letters of encouragement, the difficult, danger-filled journeys he made, and the abuse, beatings, and imprisonment he endured. Today, faithful Christians everywhere are sacrificing and suffering for Jesus, and they need your love to remain true and to grow to see Jesus more clearly. Come to Jesus, and he will teach you and strengthen your faith to reach out to your brothers and sisters.

With your anchor working in you, even the most ordinary task takes on a new meaning. You will see behind everything a greater plan. If you work alone, you may have more time to remember others in prayer; if in a crowded atmosphere, more opportunities to show the fruit of the Spirit to those all around you may arise. A

---

[177] Heb. 13:13

mother at home with little ones will sense a deeper purpose and show more of Jesus. Everything you are called to do is positive and important. Nothing is trivial in Christ's kingdom.

The precious times of exploring the purposes of God, found only in the power of the indwelling Christ, will make you long to deepen your walk. Learn to fix your eyes on Jesus, and you'll continually remember he died so he could give you real life. But never forget he also came to fulfill God's plan for the restoration of all humanity. Look to the Lord Jesus always, believing he is always working in you, and the gift of his power will flow to all around you.

Jesus told his disciples that unless a grain of wheat falls onto the earth and dies, it remains just one grain; it does not reproduce. But if it dies, it produces many others and yields a rich harvest.[178] This describes what the Savior of humankind went through in order to bring you and me eternal life in him. By dying you can help Jesus gather more precious lives for everlasting glory.

Only believe. With a strong hawser, God's glory will appear in and through you!

God's Business
Let this vignette from the life of native missionary Joy Punnoose of India inspire you. Joy was born in the more affluent southern tip of India, but after meeting Christ in a real way, he left the comforts of home and traveled by train to spread the gospel among the heavily populated regions of the north. These northerners were ethnically and religiously different from the ways of this young man from the south, but Joy loved Jesus, and he wanted to follow his leading. Yet after several years of toil and heartache, not one soul could he identify that had seen through the darkness to the light of the Lord Jesus.

Discouraged and defeated, Joy set off one day to the marketplace to buy vegetables, as he describes in his own words:

> Arriving at the market, crowded as usual with shoppers buying their fresh produce, I walked

---
[178] John 12:24 AMP

> around examining the different fruits, vegetables, and herbs. Strangely, the produce suddenly seemed to disappear, and I began to notice the people—and in a most unusual way. That day was no different from any other, but suddenly I realized I was looking at the milling throng in the market through the compassionate eyes of Jesus. The realization that I was actually seeing them with his eyes swept over my entire being as an ocean swell breaks over the rocky coastline. Tears of deep sorrow began to well up in my eyes.[179]

Joy's perspective had changed because he was now seeing life through the eyes of life's creator, Jesus Christ. His eyes were now the eyes of his Savior and Lord. The tears of the one who cried over Jerusalem two thousand years earlier now streamed from his eyes. That tearful moment opened Joy's eyes and heart, and Jesus began a work through him that led to tens of thousands of new followers of Jesus who cried tears of joy at finding the Light of life in a dark land.

Your mission is directly linked to your spiritual vision too. Close your eyes to "things," and through the eyes of Jesus you will see into the world's real needs. Look beyond people's outward circumstances, and you'll find reasons why they have become the way they are. It may take time, but the hurts, scars, and traumatic events that have shaped their lives will become evident. Those are the things Jesus sees. And that's what we will see when he takes our eyes and sees through them.

Remember Joy's account and Paul's as well when you think of your neighbor who swears or your brother in Christ who falls into sin. Purpose has to do with spiritual vision. Paul saw Jesus, and it transformed his life. No amount of self-effort could have cured his blindness; it was Jesus who did it. And oh, what mighty things began to happen when this man, filled with hatred for Jesus,

---

[179] Joy Punnoose, *Live for a Cause* (Richardson, TX: Open House Publications, 2009). Used by permission.

saw him for who he was and began living under his indwelling influence!

Paul and Joy saw Jesus, and he transformed their lives. No amount of self-effort could have done it. Feel the Lord's compassion swelling in you, and pray the Spirit will open your eyes and keep them open to see and understand all Jesus has in store for those who love him, who are called according to his purpose. Then you too can joyfully exclaim, *I once was blind, but now I see!*[180]

Conclusion

If you begin exploring the deeper purposes of God, found only in the power of the indwelling Christ, you will thirst for more of him. Faith connects you to him, and with a strong hawser, you will see the glory of God at work—in and through you.

Making a difference in lives is your purpose. Jesus showed how to invest the precious time you've been given in the greatest venture the world will ever see—the saving of lives for an eternity in glory. Displaying all the qualities of the sacrificial love of Jesus to the saved and the lost—patience, kindness, self-control, and the rest—is God's will for every Christian.

The concept of a spiritual kingdom was a new treasure to the Jews, but many did not open their eyes to see it; the indwelling Spirit was a hard teaching for them to grasp. Do you understand what God wants to do for you and through you? If you don't, but your heart is burning to know, Jesus will open your eyes, and you will recognize his ways and his presence. It may take time, but you will behold him.

Open your eyes. Look around. See the need. If Jesus lives in you and you give yourself over to his power, he will show you great and marvelous things—and you will love the world with him.

---

[180] John Newton, "Amazing Grace," *https://www.hymnal.net/en/hymn/h/313* (June 1, 2015).

CHAPTER 9
ANCHORED IN THE STORM

The blessings of abiding in Christ cannot be measured, for they place us in the heavenly realm. Live in Jesus and experience life, love, and joy as the fruit of the Spirit flows into you and out to others. Then you will be about your Father's business. What grace!

But don't be deceived. Though walking with the Lord is the best thing that will ever happen to you, many perils lie ahead. He promised as much when he said, "In the world ye shall have tribulation."[181] But the reward of being conformed to his image and always living in his presence far outweighs any adversity.

The Consequence of Sin
Everyone experiences suffering. Why? Suffering is the byproduct of living in a perfect world gone bad. Sin brought death into God's Eden and short-circuited the eternal bliss of paradise. Since that tragic day, the norm has been, "Change and decay in all around I see," according to hymnist Henry Lyte, who penned the famous hymn, *Abide with Me*. Winds of adversity constantly swirl about

---
[181] John 16:33

us: death, sickness, toil, hardship, poverty, and more. Even the beauty of nature that we sometimes attribute to the glory of God is touched by death—a dim representation of that perfect world he created. The one and only solution to this sad state of affairs is to cry out, "O Thou who changest not, abide with me."[182]

What Is Suffering?
In the world, suffering takes on two forms. Storms of mortality are the conflicts of a dying world. Then there is the suffering that comes as a result of living a life filled and guided by the Holy Spirit. These are storms of spirituality, the conflicts that Jesus experienced and calls us to.

Suffering comes in many ways, and many terms express the hurts of humanity: *testing, trial, tribulation, adversity, persecution, and others*. These terms suggest the bodily or emotional pain brought on by perfection lost. Here's a definition of *suffering* in its various forms:

> *to submit to or be forced to endure <suffer martyrdom>; to feel keenly: labor under <suffer thirst>;undergo, experience; to put up with, especially as inevitable or unavoidable*[183]

Satan lies behind all suffering. He works against everything Jesus does, and it's been that way since Eden. The fruit of the Devil's temptation in the garden was decay and death to God's perfection. Not only did Adam, Eve, and the physical world around them begin to die, but humankind's mind and soul became self-centered, ushering in spiritual death as well.

Satan was even bold enough to tempt Jesus in the wilderness. That encounter was not a direct onslaught, but one that was sly and subtle. Now, if he tempted God made man, you can be

---

[182] Henry Lyte, "Abide with Me," *https://www.hymnal.net/en/hymn/h/370* (June 1, 2015).

[183] *Merriam-Webster* Online Dictionary, *www.merriam-webster.com/dictionary/suffer* (June 28, 2015).

assured he will tempt you too. He unceasingly works through myriad worldly life-forces to lure you, little by little, away from your anchor, using even good things to tempt you to excess or error.

Our Own Sinful Nature
Satan moves in stealthy ways with the one objective of keeping you from seeing the real Jesus and abiding in him. Then he can lure you further and further from the centrality of Christ and your only hope. Without Jesus as your rock, your own human reasoning and power take over, and Satan takes the advantage as a result. Then, it's no contest. He'll win every time.

The Evil One does not want you to believe what Jesus says, nor does he want you to have life. Most assuredly, he will work with all his guile to keep you from humbly abiding in Jesus, because he does not want you to produce the effects of the fruit of the Spirit. Hatred is his goal; pride and self-centeredness his fruit. Jesus came to give life; Satan takes away life, leaving only death.

Unless you operate in the power of Christ, you continue to live in a realm where you make the choices, which can only lead downward to emptiness, futility, and ultimately death. Without Jesus, you are *power-less*. Thankfully, God loves us and refines us so the old, unfruitful, self-preserving nature takes flight, and the vibrant, fruitful nature of his *self-less* love takes the driver's seat.

Even when we ourselves do not sin, people all around us do. Family, friends, or neighbors may treat us unjustly, as well as employers and myriad others. As a result, testing and, at times, suffering come. God puts us into situations like these so we can see how we measure up.[184] Certainly such occurrences are sometimes painful, but they serve as necessary reminders that there is a higher standard to strive for—the image of Jesus.

The Death of the Body
That we will someday die a physical death is a fact none can deny; the death process actually begins the moment we are conceived.

---
[184] Heb. 12:1–11

Yet, even though our bodies encounter sickness and disease along the way, we usually give little thought to death's inevitability, especially in our younger years. However, the aging process and encountering potentially life-threatening situations bring us face-to-face with reality.

Paul illustrated a Christ-like view of mortality. He considered trials and suffering to be light, momentary afflictions since his spiritual, inward man—the real man, if you will—was all the time being renewed and becoming stronger. Not only that, this wonderful paradox of success out of suffering was producing an unending glory for Jesus because he didn't look at the temporary tests and tribulations—he looked at the eternal riches.

Inevitability of Trials

Many are shocked to learn that coming to Jesus and living a Spirit-filled life means suffering of some sort lies just down the road. What happened to the disciples as they spread out testifies to this truth. Paul and Peter's letters confirm it. The record of the faithful ones in Hebrews 11 also paints a panorama of pain and suffering through the ages up to the time it was written. Tribulation doesn't seem to line up with blessedness, but it is the way the Master and his followers went.

Keep in mind that the *blessedness* Jesus spoke of is far from the worldly definition of *happy*. Remember in chapter two where the eternal kingdom citizens would be considered as blessed: "envied, and spiritually prosperous [with life-joy and satisfaction in God's favor and salvation, *regardless of their outward conditions*]?"[185]

The world's happiness comes from getting a new car, better pay, a longer vacation, more birthday presents; the list goes on. Those, however, who live in heavenly blessedness are those who are poor in spirit, mourn over their sin, are meek, and are driven by a hunger and thirst to be filled with Jesus. They show love, are pure in heart, and they long to bring to all people the peace that passes understanding. They find true happiness in blessing others.

---

[185] pg. 12

The blessed ones are happier still because they *suffer* for Jesus—just as he suffered for them. That's right; happy are the sufferers! Though unpleasant to the flesh, Jesus told his listeners they would actually *rejoice* when they were persecuted because they would be receiving a great heavenly reward for their dedication to their Lord.[186]

Jesus said, in effect, *I love those in the world, and my Father has given me power to suffer, so they might also love.* When filled with the Spirit, we say, *Through Jesus, I love the world as he does, and my anchor gives me the power to suffer, so others might love too.*

God Refines Us to Fulfill His Purpose for Us
We may wonder, *What have I done to deserve this suffering? Why is this happening?* But don't think it strange that such events enter into your life. The love and joy of Jesus is being magnified to those around you when you face these trials with his power.[187] Such deeds strengthen the saints and amaze the world. It is the testimony of Christ at work.

God continually examines your belief in his ability to anchor you with tests, some small and seemingly insignificant, and some that are life-changing. Yet in all adversity, our willingness to trust Jesus is revealed. Through each and every trial, his goal is always to transform us into the image of his Son. The lessons he uses to get us there never cease, for there is always more to learn about his ways *and* ours, as well.

Our human nature avoids suffering of any kind. That's what makes going from a life of self to one of service difficult. But when you catch a glimpse of the deep, eternal purposes of Jesus for the glory of his kingdom, the fires begin to stir within. You may take tentative baby steps with much anxiety. But as you let go of fear and learn to cling to Christ and his power, his life becomes ingrained in your nature.

Life is a battlefield, and you are a soldier in the Lord's army. Saving and strengthening souls is your objective, so because God

---

[186] Matt. 5:10–12
[187] 1 Peter 4:12–13

loves you and needs you to achieve his purpose, he will faithfully train you to be effective in the battle. Consider all the tests for what they are—part of boot camp to help fit you for action.

Because of technology we are now global citizens, but with this change comes a lot more anxiety. We're inundated with reports of floods, fires, torrential rain, earthquakes, wars, scandals, murders, and persecutions all around the world. But behind fear lies all the uncertainty. Jesus says, *Don't worry. I care for you, so come to me. Everything you need I will give liberally to you. I am in you. Don't look around at the wind-tossed waves; look at me, and I will give you rest and peace.* Through whatever happens, he is truly all we need to have the peace for which we so desperately long.

Jesus did not just live his earthly life as an example for us and then go off to heaven to be with his Father and wait for us there. No, he lives in you to be your inner guide every step of the way, ready to work out everything you need, willing to strengthen you every day on the journey, and able to protect you through the continual valley of the shadow of death you tread here on earth. You simply need to believe him.

The Battleground

As we learned in the last chapter, be prepared to face a real battle when you choose to take Jesus at his word, one that lies on an unseen battlefield against an invisible foe. It's a spiritual conflict, but thankfully, an unseen champion lives inside.

The word *champion* once referred to a battlefield, and later it came to be used as a person who fights battles on behalf of others.[188] What a description of Jesus, who said he came "to preach the Gospel to the poor; … to heal the brokenhearted, to preach deliverance to the captives, and recovering of sight to the blind, to set at liberty them that are bruised!"[189]

Your champion is the mighty Son of God, so walk by faith, not by sight. However, beware! Just as the Emmaus disciples, you too

---

[188] *Merriam-Webster* Online Dictionary, *http://dictionary.reference.com/browse/champion* (June 1, 2015).
[189] Luke 4:18

can be blinded by ignorance, doubt, fear, or just plain unbelief. You can see, yet be blind. Whatever happens, recognize your Savior is walking with you and, in weakness and humility, ask him to fight your battles. Jesus says, *Seek my face. I will hear your plea and show myself.* Then respond, *Lord Jesus, your face will I seek.*[190] He patiently waits to bless you with a divine defense and power that will overcome every enemy.

Fighting an unseen foe is a scary proposition, and only the abiding Christ can overcome this invisible but very real enemy. That's why he came—to rescue you from what your sins deserve. Instead of plodding through life, completely helpless and vulnerable to Satan's onslaught, believe in your anchor, the one who is Alpha and Omega and the King of Kings and Lord of Lords.

Results of Faith

> I am crucified with Christ: nevertheless I live; yet not I, but Christ liveth in me: and the life which I now live in the flesh I live by the faith of the Son of God, who loved me, and gave himself for me.[191]

Like Abraham, you can be a friend of God,[192] daily communing with him and acting upon belief in Jesus even in the midst of suffering. The life that God had planned for the first man is now available as a free gift to all through the death and resurrection of the one who was, is, and forever will be. He is "the true God, and eternal life."[193]

The sufferer has learned to take Jesus at his word. Out of love he called the heavy of heart, saying, "Come to me … and I will give you rest."[194] He said to those in darkness, "I am the light of

---

[190] Ps. 27:8; Heb. 12:1–3
[191] Gal. 2:20
[192] James 2:23; John 15:14–15; *et al*
[193] 1 John 5:20
[194] Matt. 11:28

the world."[195] He stated to the fearful, "Whoever lives and believes in me will never die."[196] To the wanderers, he explained that he was the door of the sheep and the good Shepherd who would give abundant life.[197]

Those precious words hold true for you today. As you live like Jesus, you become anchored more firmly in him, so that when the trials of life befall you, you're prepared to meet them with the fruit of the Spirit. Lighthouses are anchored on solid rock, away from the tempest of the waves, and from there they send out beams of saving light. Always actively believe, and you'll be anchored in a safe haven, free from the restless seas of life.

Someone coined the term "suffering love" to define the quality of the love of Jesus. He was made perfect in suffering; he was made complete. Jesus came not to be ministered to, but to minister and to give his life. Your suffering brings out the fullness of the gifts of his spirit. Others before you lived out love, joy, peace, and patience in the face of fierce trials, and if you do the same it is rock-solid proof you are filled with a different spirit, a quiet confidence that sees through the gloom and despair of this world's struggles to an unseen Savior and a triumphant eternity at his feet. It's proof that Christ lives in you. You have been bought with a price and become a suffering servant—a bond servant who loves.

Examples of Others: Paul
Paul's life dramatically changed in a moment when a brilliant flash temporarily blinded him, and that encounter between his own sinful heart and Jesus gave this former persecutor of Christ the light of life.[198] Later, when Paul was confronted by a certain "thorn in the flesh," as he called it, he took the suffering to Jesus. Did Jesus take him out of the situation? No, but he gave Paul

---

[195] John 8:12
[196] John 11:26 NIV
[197] John 10:1–11
[198] Acts 9:1–16

something of far greater value than an escape from this trial that had caused Paul such great concern.

Instead of relief, Jesus gave Paul the gift of his mighty power to spread his love in the face of that "thorn" and any other adversity Satan might throw in his path. Christ's strength certainly was sufficient for this man of God.[199] The Lord told Paul his power was made perfect in humankind's weakness. In other words, when Christ's power works through helpless mortals, great things happen, and God gets the glory.

Paul's determination in the face of persecution and trials glorified the strength of Jesus. He stated that he actually gloried in tribulation because out of the trials of life, the patience to pursue and display an abiding life was formed and nurtured. Where patience reigns continually, experience and wisdom grow. Then hope blossoms and springs into eternal blessings.[200] Ever an encourager, Paul taught that the believer's hope for glory was "Christ in you."[201] And his own testimony was "Christ lives in me."[202]

Was Paul a super-hero? No. He was obedient to what the Lord Jesus requires of all his followers. Jesus was his anchor, and he was determined not to drift from the presence of his Rock.

Peter—Before and After

Peter also was acquainted with suffering, and it is no coincidence that the Holy Spirit has used the lives of both Peter and Paul down through the centuries as examples for those who would face tribulation. Peter had been an independent boaster, but Jesus changed him into a meek servant. He was not only victorious through the imprisonments and other trials he endured because of the name of Jesus—he also left hope and encouragement for other fellow sufferers by way of his letters.

What was Peter's secret? Though he had walked and talked

---

[199] 2 Cor. 12:7–10
[200] Rom. 5:3–5
[201] Col. 1:27
[202] Gal. 2:20 NIV

with Jesus in the past, his life was revolutionized when the Holy Spirit of Christ entered his heart, for now Jesus lived *inside* Peter! He had become a man known for his love.

Driven by the Spirit to comfort others, Peter began his first letter to suffering saints scattered far and wide on a note of encouragement. He said that their faith in Jesus was more precious than gold and was tested by suffering so that it would become even more pure. Seeing the Spirit work through them would then increase their hope of being with Jesus forever: the greater the heat, the keener the anticipation of heaven.[203]

Peter so clearly defined the value and purpose of all believers: "You are a chosen race, a royal priesthood, a dedicated nation, [God's] own purchased, special people, that you may set forth the wonderful deeds *and d*isplay the virtues and perfections of Him who called you out of darkness into His marvelous light."[204] They were chosen to live Christ and show his love to the world; they were suffering for Jesus. Jesus set the example, and believers were to follow his steps, just as Peter himself was doing.

Suffering in Other Lands
Brothers and sisters in the developing countries and Muslim-ruled lands are just as precious to God as you are, and most of them were born into suffering; they've never known a life without poverty, hunger, and often, persecution. Their empty religions promise paradise but give only deception and darkness. But when they find Jesus they find peace, light, love, and a reason to live. Yet that decision alone may bring persecution to their doorstep. Entire families may be ostracized from their villages and forced to live as nomads. Then there is the physical persecution: beatings, burnings, torture, imprisonment, and killings.

How are they able to endure the radical suffering of being rejected by family, friends, community—their entire social and former religious base? How can they call themselves *blessed* in the face of hatred? Echoing Paul's bold assertion, they *glory* in

---

[203] 1 Peter 1:1–16
[204] 1 Peter 2:9 AMP

persecution because they then can display the power of Jesus to love their brethren in the face of such dire circumstances. As a result, others notice and the gospel of Jesus spreads like wildfire in these danger zones.

Testimonies from saints in developing nations are striking and power-packed. In the midst of poverty and persecution, though their own families may turn them out, the fruit of the Spirit works mightily among them. The love of Jesus abounds, and so do acts of kindness. Meeting the needs of their fellow believers becomes a joy. The zeal of Jesus to reach the lost becomes their driving force, even though torture is around every corner. As trials increase, so does the love. Hallelujah, what a Savior!

The purpose behind persecution is dear to the Lord's heart. He commands us to identify with the persecuted saints all over the world so closely that we are virtually suffering with them, even though we do not partake of the physical struggles ourselves.[205] They are part of his body, bear his suffering, and need our prayers.

Persecution in Developed Countries
It's sad that many professing Christians are so lost in comfort that they are actually repulsed at the thought of persecution—while the One with the nail-pierced hands and pierced side longs to be their abiding Lord and teach them his ways. Christianity in the West has drifted so far from what Jesus says that many even consider deviant behavior as being acceptable. But when persecution is mentioned, they recoil in horror and fear, blind to all the passages of Scripture that promise suffering.

Complacent Christians pay little attention to the cost paid by brothers and sisters in hostile lands. However, there has been a recent quantum leap in the kind of persecution the Bible speaks about in the wealthier nations. The forces of hell are now aiming frontal attacks at comfortable Christianity, and soon believers will have to either take a stand and suffer the consequences, deny their faith, or try to walk the middle of the road—which is the same as denial.

---

[205] Heb. 13:3

Do you remember the great earthquake that rocked Japan a few years ago? The waters of the tidal waves (or tsunamis) it generated were even a more destructive force to that island nation than the tremors themselves. Video images of walls of water surging ashore were at the same time riveting and terrifying.

One such video was taken by someone standing on the roof of a multistory building in a coastal town. The scene that unfolded below them was surreal and incomprehensible. In the distance, the surge of the sea breached the shore, and water soon rushed down streets that ran toward the building, not as a giant wave but as the opening of an irrigation gate in a farmer's field.

Soon water had crept over the streets of the entire city. Then its level began rising higher, and as it did so, the unstoppable force lifted up objects and began carrying them along—first trash cans, then cars. The waters rose higher still, and soon small structures floated by and then entire houses. After a while, the taller buildings became islands in the sea.

This tragic scene reminded me of another disaster thousands of years earlier. No one then was expecting a flood, but at least they were given one opportunity to escape it. However, only a few heeded the warning that preceded it. Those floodwaters first rose enough to float Noah's ark and continued to rise. Eventually they rose above the mountains until there was nothing visible but the sky, the water, and the ark. This did not happen in a moment's time, but eventually the entire earth was covered with water, and the only living souls that survived were in that ship—those who heeded the call.

Our planet is being overwhelmed by a tsunami of epic proportions. Even the great flood of Noah's time cannot compare to the devastation happening today. The floodwaters have been rising for centuries, and soon there will be nowhere to run, nowhere to hide. There will be no place on earth that will be physically safe. But just as he did thousands of years ago when the floodwaters were released, our loving Father has provided a safe haven, a solid rock.

Your only hope for reaching the acceptance and usefulness

you were created to experience is in the One who is the captain of your salvation. Jesus stands calm and firm in the midst of the ocean waves and in the beating winds, assuring you that all is well with your soul and that, despite the tempest, you are being used according to his plan.

For the more affluent, this present age presents a crossroad: follow the suffering Jesus, or compromise in order to evade persecution and keep your way of life. If Jesus is your anchor, you will be tempted, mocked, and rejected, but you will have his indwelling power to overcome whatever happens—*if* you deny yourself, believe, and follow him. Remember, to live is Christ; to die is gain.[206] Which is better—becoming like Jesus, or getting a new car? Loving others by showing patience, gentleness, and kindness, or going on a long vacation? In other words, focus on the real blessings.

Jesus Christ is your *soul solution* to both weather the storms and understand their purpose. He knows best how to work out things for your good and his glory. Since he is love, he knows everything will work together for good—if you love him and are living according to his purpose.[207] It's easy to look at suffering as a kind of punishment. But from a godly perspective, trials become a blessing when these experiences mold you into the image of Jesus.

Successful suffering for Jesus hinges on what your hope is. We'll find out more in the next chapter.

---

[206] Phil. 1:21
[207] Rom. 8:28

CHAPTER 10

ANCHORED IN HOPE

In God's realm, hope is the confident expectation of someday experiencing what lies ahead in his unseen eternal kingdom. Those who have this heavenly vision exhibit visible proof that God's invisible love is genuine because hope in the promises of spending an eternity with Jesus grows and grows. This assurance also produces more and more love for the saints and the lost.

If you know and follow Jesus, you have already been blessed beyond measure at this point in your life. Your sins are forgiven, you have a new life, and Christ is abiding. You are accepted, loved, and entrusted with a purpose. You feel the joy of answered prayer. But all that is only a foretaste to the blessedness beyond this mortal life.

What do you want most? The greatest blessing waiting for you in heaven isn't a mansion or walking streets paved with gold. It is being with Jesus for eternity. The thought of living with our Lord and Savior in a perfect world forever should—and must—motivate everything you do.

Read this book again when you finish these final pages, and as you do, concentrate on what Jesus has done for you. Out of love he left heaven to die for you, lived as a religious outcast to teach you how to live, loved everyone to show you how to love, and served even those who wronged him to teach you how to serve. He died to give you life, sent his Spirit to be your tutor, abides in you to be your strength, and promises to embrace you in heaven. Imagine sitting with him on his throne! He will take away all suffering. No heartaches, no pain, and no tears!

All power has been given to this Lamb of God who takes away the sin of the world. He is the beginning, center, and completion of God's magnificent plan—truly the Alpha and the Omega. *The Amplified Bible* paraphrases Romans 11:36 this way: "For all things originate with Him and come from Him; all things live through Him, and all things center in and tend to consummate and to end in Him. To Him be glory forever! Amen."

Jesus Is Our Hope
Jesus is the living hope Peter speaks of.[208] He is alive, and if you truly long to abide with him forever, these thoughts will both stir and comfort your heart as nothing else can. And, praise God, you can have a living foretaste of eternal, divine glory this and every moment until that day when your faith becomes sight arrives!

All along, Christ's calling has had as its purpose the exaltation of the Lord Jesus Christ and being anchored in him for his work of bringing the world into his presence in glory. He is the bridegroom, we are the bride. The hymn, "The Sands of Time" pictures perfectly the eternal glory we will witness in our "Immanuel's land" when we see Jesus, the spotless Lamb of God once slain, and our anchor, face-to-face:

> The Bride eyes not her garment, but her dear Bridegroom's face;
> I will not gaze at glory but on my King of grace.

---

[208] 1 Peter 1:3

Not at the crown He giveth, but on His pierced hand;
The Lamb is all the glory of Immanuel's land.[209]

Your task here and now is to bring glory to your Bridegroom. That's why it is crucial, dear friend, to be rooted in him. Being rooted in Christ is essential for doing his work, for he is the center of everything here and throughout eternity. We are his hands, feet, and mouth his bride. We are his body, he is the head.

Abraham struck out for a land he had never seen because God told him to go and that he would lead him there. Jesus has given you his promise that he will lead you to heaven, even though you cannot see beyond this life. If you always look beyond the darkness of this sinful world and see Jesus, you can overcome everything the world throws at you.

Trials and temptations will not disappear, of that you can be sure. But with eternity in view, you can be an overcomer and live a life of purpose and promise. Jesus, the anchor of our hope, is cheering you on and giving strength as you meet the struggles that come your way. He always understands what you are facing, for he faced it himself victoriously and destroyed Satan's power to harm you.[210] You don't have to recite long verses or say mighty prayers. Reach out to Jesus in the midst of testing, and you can rest assured the promise he made to make it through will be kept in his time and by his method.

Aa anchor is let down from a ship to hold that vessel in a certain location, but that doesn't mean the ship will not move about. If there are large waves, the ship will still turn and bob up and down, but it will be held in place. Likewise, if you are anchored in Christ, suffering may strike, but his promises still will not fail.

The Lord wants to anchor your senses and your emotions in him so that you will hold fast and not give up. You have a task to

---

[209] Annie R. Cousin, *The Sands of Time are Sinking*, http://www.sermonaudio.com/hymn_details.asp?PID=*immanuelsland* (June 1, 2015).
[210] Heb. 2:14–18

fulfill, one that will take the power of his abiding fruit to carry out. You may have first trusted in Christ in the past, but now it's time to learn that Jesus is sending you to face tribulation for his glory.

You and I will be raised to a never-ending life, just as Jesus was raised from the dead and received eternal glory. We live with great expectations because we have a priceless inheritance waiting in heaven, pure and undefiled and beyond the reach of change and decay. Even though you endure many trials, feel truly blessed; there is wonderful joy ahead!

Your Focus
This hope is a spiritual one not connected to a person, such as a spouse, pastor, or friend. If Jesus Christ is not your eternal focus, you may get temporary relief from your struggles elsewhere, but you'll end up worse off than you were before. If you hope in your money, you will eventually be disappointed because it cannot buy loving acceptance, nor can it bring true happiness. If it's in a person, that person will let you down sooner or later. That new car will lose its distinctive smell and get old. But Jesus will never grow old, nor will he ever fail or disappoint. Put your confidence in him, and he will bring everything he promised to pass.

Perhaps you've made the mistake of asking the Lord to bless you materially so you would have more to spend on comfort and pleasure. God may allow you to have an abundance of this world's treasure, but through it he finds out where your priorities lie. God will definitely shower you with precious riches, but his riches are those found in his Son. Everything God does and gives is part of his plan to conform you to Jesus.

Consider this: with only a few coins, George Müller of England founded Christian-based orphanages that took in many English children in the late 1800s and early 1900s and gave them a home, food, clothing, and an education. How could he accomplish all this? A true man of faith, he firmly believed God would provide everything without mentioning it to anyone but God alone. And

God met every need. George died leaving a mere pittance in his estate, but he had provided the way to eternal riches for thousands and had himself gained the treasure of heaven.

Remember, the earth is the Lord's and everything in it. He has a purpose for what he gives you, and it's not for you to spend on yourself to be comfortable—it's to further his kingdom. At some time and in some way, someone sacrificed so that eventually you could hear the good news of Jesus and his love and be saved. That person may have lived long ago, but an act of selfless generosity on his or her part started a chain of events that eventually included your life, even though that person may have never met you. That person didn't comfort him- or herself; that person comforted you.

Hope in the Unseen

> For we were saved in this hope, but hope that is seen is not hope; for why does one still hope for what he sees? But if we hope for what we do not see, then we eagerly wait for it with perseverance.[211]

Truly, you have an anchor that is sure and steadfast, but unless you patiently endure, you will never experience his comfort. God may touch everything in your life to refine and strengthen you: your prayer life, your children, your husband or wife, your health, your car, even your concept of church. Abraham patiently endured through many trials, and he and his wife, Sarah, were given a child in their old age that represented the beginning of the descendants the Lord had promised.

This hope of heaven is not a wish you think might come true; it's not a longing for your car to start when you know the battery is low. Hebrews says our steadfast hope is in the One who suffered death, went behind the veil, and opened heaven for all to have eternal life in his name. When he did, he took away all reasons for fear. Believing in his abiding presence replaces fear with hope

---

[211] Rom. 8:23–24 NKJV

and joy. The Holy Spirit makes up for our weakness and insecurity with the mighty power of Jesus.[212]

Don't dwell on the struggles threatening you, but instead on what you are looking forward to. The Lord is working, even when the situation looks the darkest. Though you may be walking through the valley of the shadow of death, Jesus is leading you on to his banqueting table.[213]

Confidently state, *I love you, Lord, my safeguard. Give me a contrite heart, one that is resolved and fixed. When I get into a difficult situation in life, I will not search for help because I know you are inside, for I believe your promise that you would never leave or forsake me. I know we will someday be together face-to-face, and I will even be like you. And since I want others to share that joy, I forsake my own selfish way so I can be constantly busy doing your will.*[214]

Hope will grow strong if you don't dwell on the negative aspects of life. Instead, love Jesus with all your heart, mind, soul, and strength, and your neighbors as yourself.[215] When Jesus fills you with himself, you will even love your enemies, though they may mistreat you. As you spend more time with him, you will get to know him better—a powerful motivation to always be in his presence. Your hope will produce a stronger desire to see others meet you at the feet of the Savior.

Regardless of what you are going through, your anchor never changes. But you'll never know how strong he is until you have been tried and tested. You can say you love Jesus, you'll do anything for him, and you'll always follow him, no matter how hard the road. But it's not until the road gets rough that your words are proven. Then people who may have never read the Bible will see Jesus in you, if you pass the tests.

Faith is the assurance of things hoped for.[216] *The Amplified Bible* says it is the conviction of their reality, the assurance that things in

---

[212] Heb. 6:19–20
[213] Ps. 23:4; Song 2:4
[214] 1 John 3:2–3
[215] Luke 10:27
[216] Heb. 11:1

the future will come to pass. Without it, you cannot please God.[217] In a season of suffering and trials, it's easy to think nothing is happening. Keep your hope on Jesus regardless, because he will bring to pass what he told you. You know he can bring good out of it, so wait. Consider for a moment how the faith of two men turned a troublesome situation into a time of rejoicing.

Hope Tested
Paul and Silas were in prison, but they were being used by God, and they were doing his will. Despite their chains, they rejoiced in Jesus and prayed. They were anything but hopeless. On the contrary, each was confident in the Lord. Why? Because both had an eternal perspective and saw beyond the moment. They didn't require the things of the world to be happy or feel a need to do something fun or entertaining to find their purpose. These brothers in Christ rejoiced at midnight in the middle of a prison because they looked beyond their outward circumstances and saw Jesus—and that was enough.[218]

The Bible also says Moses endured suffering because he saw him who is invisible.[219] And that's where faith brings you as well—to the One who is invisible. And when you are going through the trial, you hear Jesus say, "I will never leave you nor forsake you."[220]

God is not simply a higher power; he is all powerful. Jesus said to his Father, "Nevertheless … thy will be done,"[221] and that's where God is leading you. Trials and tribulations bring death to the old man, making your weaknesses and inability to control the situation more obvious. But, praise God, the new man equipped with the indwelling power of Jesus can take over. You no longer need to look to yourself for relief or for a solution to the test—you look to the one whose strength is greater than yours and do his will.

---

[217] Heb. 11:6
[218] Acts 16:16–34
[219] Heb. 11:27
[220] Heb. 13:5
[221] Luke 22:42

There in the prison, Paul and Silas couldn't do anything on their own about their predicament, but Jesus was there, unseen, with them. They *could*, however, praise God—which they did. Then the earth quaked, the prison doors flew open, and they were free.

Why were Paul and Silas jailed? So that they could bring the good news of the Lord Jesus Christ to their astonished jailer. And as a result of that testing time for Paul and Silas, that amazed man and his family met the Lord Jesus Christ and were saved.

The Lord has "jailers" he wants to lead you to as well, and he will use any situation he sees best to make your paths cross. The Bible says your "light affliction" is but for a moment, but the inward man is renewed day after day.[222] As you carry the testimony of the Lord through your seasons of suffering, your faith is strengthened, and you draw ever closer to your anchor.

Amy Carmichael spent most of her life in India rescuing young girls from a life of sordid slavery and showing them the love of Jesus. But an accident left her an invalid for the last twenty years of her life. A prolific writer of books, spiritual-laden notes, letters, and poetry, she spent those days of debilitation encouraging others with her pen. Rather than seek her own deliverance, these lines from her eloquent poem, "Make Me Thy Fuel," shows that her desire to serve Jesus kept burning through her trial:

> From all that dims Thy Calvary,
> O Lamb of God, deliver me.
> Give me the love that leads the way,
> The faith that nothing can dismay,
> The hope no disappointments tire,
> The passion that will burn like fire;
> Let me not sink to be a clod:
> Make me Thy fuel, Flame of God.[223]

---

[222] 2 Cor. 4:15–18

[223] Carmichael, Amy. *Mountain Breezes*. Fort Washington, PA: Christian Literature Crusade, 1999.

Your hope is the steadfast anchor for your soul.[224] Don't stop believing! Make the hard choices, just as Jesus did. Let love lead your way on the road to eternal glory and persistently press toward heaven, regardless of what is going on around you. Don't be moved, and always be on fire in the work of the Lord.[225] If you build your hope on him, your flame will never flicker and die.

---

[224] Heb. 6:19
[225] 1 Cor. 15:58

CONCLUSION

Where do you stand with Jesus? You cannot merely tread water. Will your union with him be strong enough when the fierce winds of pressure, chaos, destruction, persecution, and more threaten to destroy you? Satan intends for such trials to rock your boat, drive you to fear, and block the fruit of the Spirit from doing its work. But when you admit you are helpless, you are then strong—if only you abide in him.

Jesus truly cares for you. Regardless of the outward circumstances looming before you, believe what he says, cast all your care on him, and his wisdom and love will pour into your heart. Standing tall in the storms of life will prove it—both to yourself and to a lost and helpless world.

Without the anchor, you will be carried into riptides, whirlpools, and over waterfalls that will pull you under and drown you in the misery of the world.[226] With Jesus, your spirit will soar like an eagle, away from the depths threatening to engulf you and upward to an endless horizon of glorious opportunities to serve. Whoever first said, "It's not about me!" was right on. It is about others, but above all it's about the Lord because when you love others, you prove God's way is the right way. Always believe Jesus is your anchor, Rock, captain, first mate, and Savior rolled into one. Abide in him continually,

---

[226] Heb. 2:1–3

beholding his face; you'll be yoked together with him and transformed into his likeness.[227]

Who else but God knows exactly what you need to enhance your character? Put him in control of everything—your time, talents, finances, etc.—because he longs for you to realize that being a servant is the best thing that could happen to you. After all, the Son of God said he himself came not to be served but to serve and to give his life. If you are a servant and put your life on the line, then you are abiding in Christ and are becoming like him. In Christ's realm, humble servants are the children of the King!

Because God loved the world, our Lord Jesus came seeking and saving the lost. That was his purpose, and it is your purpose as well, your business. When people use the word *business,* they almost always mean making money or buying something. But the word is actually derived from *busyness* and means "full of activity, industrious." That's the example Jesus left for us. He was always on the move, showing love in its various forms.

Charles Dickens's unforgettable miser, Ebenezer Scrooge, knew nothing of love, except love for money. One Christmas Eve, Scrooge received a visit from three apparitions sent to show him the kind of life he had lived and the reward to come for his lack of compassion and ignoring the tremendous needs he met daily. The second of these spirits, the ghost of Christmas present, appeared to show him how much kindness, compassion, and goodwill his true nature was lacking. A jovial, friendly giant who loved people, the messenger cried out to a cowering Scrooge standing at the doorway: "Come in and know me better, man … You have never seen the like of me before!"[228]

Engrave this principle in your heart and mind: Humankind is your Lord Jesus Christ's business, and your sovereign King stipulates that you make it your business too. Jesus has shown you how to invest the precious time you've been given in the greatest

---

[227] 2 Cor. 3:18
[228] Charles Dickens, *A Christmas Carol, http://www.gutenberg.org/files/46/46-h/46-h.htm* (June 1, 2015).

venture the world will ever see—the saving of lives for an eternity in glory. Yes, displaying all the qualities of the sacrificial love of Jesus to the saved and the lost—patience, kindness, self-control, and the rest—is *definitely* your business.

Our Lord refers to overcomers as those who "keep my works unto the end."[229] Persevere in hope and love and you will have a crown of life and not be hurt by eternal death. Jesus will confess your name to the Father, and you will be ushered into the New Jerusalem and receive a new name. There you will partake of the hidden manna and be privileged to drink from the fountain of life and eat of the Tree of Life. Finally, you will sit with Jesus on his throne forever.[230]

What a privilege, what grace is bestowed on those who were once "alienated and enemies in [their minds] by wicked works!"[231] The promise made by God and Jesus to fill your hungry, thirsting soul will be realized in its fullness if you overcome in this life. Such is the blessed hope of those who do not seek for purpose of life in the things of this world.

The book of Hebrews refers to people on the overcomers' road as strangers and pilgrims—literally aliens. Unlike most of those around them, they long for a better country, a kingdom that cannot be moved, a city that is to come—the heavenly Jerusalem. Such people are on a journey to a better place. They, like Moses, suffer with the people of God in this life, esteem the reproach of Christ in this life, and forsake the world in this life.[232]

Why do these "foreigners" endure such hardship? Because they see him who is invisible in this life and look ahead to their reward in eternity. They know beyond any shadow of doubt that when Jesus appears, they will be like him, for they will see him as he is.[233] Their testimony in everlasting glory will be that "they overcame ... by the blood of the lamb and by the word of their

---

[229] Rev. 2:26
[230] Rev. 2:26; 2:7, 10–11, 17; 3:5, 12, 21
[231] Col. 1:21
[232] Heb. 11:13–16, 23–27
[233] 1 John 3:2

testimony; and they loved not their lives [on this earth] unto the death."[234]

The saints who suffered in the past looked not at troubles but forward to Jesus, the author and perfecter of their faith. They saw the glorified, victorious Jesus as the abiding life-giver. Being filled with his Spirit, they found that all fullness dwelled in him. This assurance then led them in victory through all the trials they met. They loved and served to the end, just as their Lord had done. And they too became overcomers.

At the beginning of this book I quoted the first line of the beloved hymn, "Take My Life and Let it Be,"[235] written by Frances Havergal, one who suffered much in her rather brief life. Read her entire poem below and the sentiments following each thought, and reflect on where you stand with Jesus:

Take my life, and let it be consecrated, Lord, to Thee.
You gave me new life, real life. Use it, Lord, to fulfill my purpose in your kingdom of light and love.

Take my moments and my days; let them flow in ceaseless praise.
Lord, you know that my moments and days silently, swiftly turn into weeks and years. May every moment, as many as you give, be spent bringing you precious fruit.

Take my hands, and let them move at the impulse of Thy love.
Saturate my thoughts, words, and actions with your love so I may glorify your name.

Take my feet, and let them be swift and beautiful for Thee.
Use each fleeting hour to nurture the vast, white fields ready for harvest.

---

[234] Rev. 12:11
[235] Frances Havergal, "Take My Life and Let it Be," 7

Take my voice, and let me sing, always, only, for my King.
You are my strength and my song. May the melodies of your Spirit bring peace to a weary world.

Take my lips, and let them be filled with messages from Thee.
Just as you spoke the love of your Father, may I proclaim only your glory. Speak, for your servant is listening and eager to pass it on.

Take my silver and my gold; not a mite would I withhold.
Freely I have received. May I freely invest your blessing in eternal treasures.

Take my intellect, and use every power as Thou shalt choose.
You are wisdom. Direct my mind to bring glory to you.

Take my will, and make it Thine; it shall be no longer mine.
Remake my self-pleasing into your self-sacrificing, suffering servant.

Take my heart, it is Thine own; it shall be Thy royal throne.
Abide in me, Lord. Keep me from forgetting for one moment that you are reigning there.

Take my love; my Lord, I pour at Thy feet its treasure-store.
Master, I love you, for you are love. Radiate your love through whatever I say or do to whomever I meet.

Take myself, and I will be ever, only, all for Thee.
Lord Jesus, all of me is yours, at this moment and every moment. Use me as you see best.

To be consecrated is to be dedicated to a sacred purpose. Dedicate yourself to Jesus, live in him, and all adversities thrown in your path will become stepping stones to a life of love and usefulness. Therein lies the only answer to successfully facing the sin and decay, the fear and doubting, the insecurity and uncertainty, and the sorrow and suffering you experience and see all around you.

The abiding love of Jesus is ever-present and stormproof. It isn't fickle, leaving and running after new loves. It remains true. Jesus implores you at this moment, "As the Father hath loved me, so have I loved you: *continue ye in my love.*"[236]

In closing, consider this testimonial from Paul, the apostle, regarding his zeal for Jesus—one you should make a motto for your life:

My determined purpose is ...

- that I may know Him [that I may progressively become more deeply and intimately acquainted with Him, perceiving and recognizing and understanding the wonders of His Person more strongly and more clearly] ...
- and that I may in that same way come to know the power outflowing from His resurrection [which it exerts over believers] ...
- and that I may so share His sufferings as to be continually transformed [in spirit into His likeness even] to His death.[237]

The secret of Paul's strength was his determined purpose to know Jesus, be like him, suffer for him, and share eternity with him. Paul really believed!

Don't be left without a rudder, adrift on the sea of eternity. Trade in your searching and uncertainty for a deep and abiding relationship with Jesus, and in return, the calm serenity of being anchored to the King of love, even amid the churning chaos of life, will be yours. Overcome yourself and every looming mountain. Yoked with Jesus and moving by his powerful impulse, the hurting people of the world will become your business. "Be strong in the

---

[236] John 15:9 (emphasis mine)
[237] Phil. 3:7–14 AMP

Lord, and in the power of his might."[238] Get to know him better and discover you've never seen the like of him before! Then, you will know you are loved, and you will love the world. Your quest for acceptance and purpose will be fulfilled!

God told Abraham to leave his country and go to an unknown land. Jesus told Paul to leave the pomp and prestige of the world and go to the Gentiles. Today, you and I are called to get out of the world's system, become aliens, and head for a better country where the Lamb of God lives.

My friends, the day of this world is closing; darkness is drawing near. Call out to the One who is walking with you, *Abide in me!* Then, on that great tomorrow, you will fellowship with the Lamb, eat from the Tree of Life, and drink from the Water of Life—you and the saints whom you helped to heaven.

Even so, come Lord Jesus.[239] But until he does, "Grow in grace, and in the knowledge of [your] Lord and Savior Jesus Christ. To him be glory both now and forever."[240]

Make Jesus your anchor today and always.

Amen.

---

[238] Eph. 6:10
[239] Rev. 22:20
[240] 2 Peter 3:18

www.ingramcontent.com/pod-product-compliance
Lightning Source LLC
Chambersburg PA
CBHW020007050426
42450CB00005B/356